ROMANCE MONOGRAPHS, INC.

Number 15

THE LIFE AFTER BIRTH:
IMAGERY IN
SAMUEL BECKETT'S TRILOGY

ROMANCE MONOGRAPHS, INC.
Number 15

THE LIFE AFTER BIRTH:
IMAGERY IN
SAMUEL BECKETT'S TRILOGY

BY

PHILIP H. SOLOMON

UNIVERSITY, MISSISSIPPI
ROMANCE MONOGRAPHS, INC.

1 9 7 5

Library of Congress Cataloging in Publication Data

Solomon, Philip.
    The life after birth.

    (Romance monographs; no. 15)
    Bibliography: p.

    1. Beckett, Samuel, 1906-   —Style. I. Title.
PQ2603.E378Z84   843'.9'14   75-11625

For my Mother and Father, and for Risa and Elycia

ACKNOWLEDGMENTS

I wish to thank Grove Press, Inc. for permission to quote from Three Novels *(Copyright © 1955, 1956, 1958 by Grove Press, Inc.) and from* Proust *(All Rights Reserved). Some material from chapters I, II, and V has previously appeared in* Forum for Modern Language Studies, Australian Journal of French Studies, *and* French Review *respectively. I am grateful to their editors for permission to reprint.*

I would like to express my appreciation to Professor Alan J. Clayton of Tufts University for his help and encouragement in the publication of this book, and, above all, to Professor Germaine Brée of the University of Wisconsin, under whose guidance I first began to study Beckett's novels.

Is there a life after birth?

Anonymous

CONTENTS

Page

INTRODUCTION   13

  I. THE SHRINKING SPACE   21

 II. JOURNEY WITHOUT END   54

III. THE SOFT LIFE   80

IV. LIGHT FALLS   94

 V. A BECKETT BESTIARY   114

CONCLUSION   144

BIBLIOGRAPHY   152

REFERENCES

Quotations from the English translation of the trilogy have been taken from *Three Novels by Samuel Beckett: Molloy, Malone Dies, The Unnamable* (New York: Grove Press, Black Cat Books, 1965). References to the original French are from *Molloy* (1951), *Malone meurt* (1951), *L'Innommable* (1953), published in Paris by the Editions de Minuit. Also cited are *Proust* (New York: Grove Press, 1957) and *Murphy* (New York: Grove Press, 1957).

INTRODUCTION

IN HIS EXCELLENT INTRODUCTION TO *Samuel Beckett: A Collection of Critical Essays,* Martin Esslin, the editor of the collection, devotes his attention not only to Beckett's works but to Beckett's critics as well. Recognizing the validity of a multiplicity of critical approaches to Beckett's writings — so long as they refuse the "cut and dried results" of facile identifications and the imposition of philosophical systems upon the texts — Esslin remarks, nonetheless, that the "challenging task for the critic is the uncovering of structural principles, the outline of the main design, which must be present in an *oeuvre* in which the concept of the games that the consciousness must play to fill the void is of such importance. Games have rules that can be deduced from observing the players. And only when the rules are known to the spectators can they fully enter into and share the excitement of the players. The elucidation of the structural principles governing each of Beckett's works is therefore . . . a function for the critic which should help the reader to achieve some degree of communication with the writer and to enter into the experience he is seeking to convey." [1]

Esslin also examines the evolution of a corpus of criticism. The critic — no less than the artist — does not, should not, work in a vacuum. Each critic reflects in what

---

[1] Martin Esslin, Introduction, in *Samuel Beckett: A Collection of Critical Essays,* ed. Martin Esslin (Englewood Cliffs, New Jersey: Spectrum Books, 1965), pp. 11-12.

he writes, explicitly or implicitly, approvingly or disap-
provingly, the studies of those critics who have preceded
him. "An individual thinker's work," Esslin notes, "will
eventually be seen as the movement of a living, constantly
changing organic tradition." This "movement," this evolution, will act as a filter of sorts, "eliminating the irrelevant,
insensitive, or factually mistaken critical evaluations from
the body of an organic tradition that is constantly forming
and renewing itself." [2]

One might argue that these remarks are critical com-
monplaces. Perhaps so — but are they any the less valid
for it? These first principles certainly needed to be stated
in 1965, when Esslin's Introduction was published, a time
when each new book on Beckett was mapping hitherto un-
explored regions, a time when one could scarcely speak
about a "tradition" of Beckett criticism. [3] "Outlines," "de-
signs," and "rules" were called for in order to lay down a
critical foundation, create a new and specific vocabulary,
and properly shape the perceptions of readers and critics
alike. In the relatively brief period of time that has elapsed
since the appearance of Esslin's Introduction there has
been, of course, an extraordinary growth in the quantity
of Beckett criticism. This growth and the direction it has
taken make Esslin's words no less pertinent now than they
were in 1965, for they reveal not only how far Beckett criticism has come but that it has reached an important turning point.

Any attempt to establish an overall evaluation of the
many books on Beckett is, obviously, fraught with dangers
— summary judgements and self-aggrandizement not being
the least among them. There always exists the possibility
that the next volume on Beckett will shatter the old as-
sumptions and lead to a radical shift in critical perspective. Then, too, Beckett himself has not yet ceased to write
and to publish. We may not be "at the end of our sur-

    [2] *Ibid.,* p. 13.
    [3] See the bibliography at the end of the *Collection of Critical
Essays,* p. 182.

prises" — as were, or thought they were, those critics who believed that *The Unnamable* marked the limit of Beckett's creativity.

Despite these risks, I maintain that a sufficient number of broad, comprehensive studies of Beckett's works have already appeared. They have more than adequately answered Esslin's challenge; and the accumulated opinions of readers and critics have, with the passage of time, discerned those that have answered it best.[4] The moment has come for a proliferation of book or monograph-length (as opposed to the limited space of an article) second-generation studies of Beckett. To return to Esslin's game metaphor, there has been enough preoccupation with the "rules" — we must now turn our attention to the finer points of how the game is played.

Having done his research and assimilated these basic and essential books — whose views will constitute his point of departure, views he will subsequently confirm, or modify, or perhaps reject as he fleshes them out — the second-generation critic can now narrow his scope to a more limited subject and, from this perspective, focus upon one or a small number of Beckett's works. And I believe it will be by means of a sustained, close examination of the text — considered in its literal sense as a weaving composed of many interconnected threads — by means of an analysis that eschews inclusiveness for depth and wealth of detail that the second- generation critic will offer new insights into the material he treats and add a new dimension to the "tradition" in which he participates.[5]

The need for this sort of scrutiny is particularly relevant to the study of Beckett's novels because of their length but it is certainly pertinent to other genres as well. The virtual neglect of the *Texts for Nothing* is the most conspicuous

---

[4] The reader will readily discern some of my own preferences on the basis of the critics I quote.

[5] Robert Harrison's monograph *Samuel Beckett's Murphy: A Critical Excursion* (Athens, Georgia, University of Georgia Press), published in 1968, is an excellent example of a second-generation study.

example of the way in which an individual work, and, in this case, one that is of crucial importance in the evolution of Beckett's fiction, can be glossed over time and again in books devoted to more general considerations.

It is with this lack of second-generation studies of Beckett's works in mind that I have undertaken to analyze certain images in the trilogy. Although one can treat each volume separately, the three novels considered in the order in which Beckett conceived and composed them reveal a particular development and unity. My aim will be, then, to "elucidate" each of the novels and the trilogy as a whole through a study of imagery.

I have chosen to examine five categories of images in the trilogy: space, movement, softness, light, and animals. These images have been selected because of their frequency and because it is through them that the three dimensions of the trilogy — existential, epistemological, aesthetic — are crystallized. In their development, extension, interrelationship, and ultimate harmony they reveal, within the framework they define, the nature of Beckett's vision of the world and the extraordinary consistency of its forms.

In this study I shall not be concerned with the formal structure of individual images. As my point of departure I shall assume that the images of the trilogy take the form of a certain type of metaphor. By metaphor I simply mean the figure of speech in which what is given stands for and refers to something else, what Wellek and Warren term "presentation and representation." [6] As Neal Oxenhandler notes, Beckett's imagery, like that of many other modern writers, is relatively "unassigned"; that is to say, the second term of the metaphor, the "representation," is usually not given in the figure in question. The reader discovers what is being represented by relating the "presentation" to the pattern or patterns to which it may be attached: "The second term of the metaphor is read back into the work by

---

[6] René Wellek and Austin Warren, *Theory of Literature*, 2nd ed. (New York: Harvest Books, 1956), p. 177.

structural and mythico-symbolic devices of plot and characterization."[7] In the case of Beckett, we must add to this last statement a certain concept of the self which, as we shall see, provides an essential framework of reference for "reading back" into a given "presentation."

Let us take a somewhat familiar kinetic image from *Molloy* and very briefly see how this process of "reading back" operates. Toward the end of his journey, Molloy crosses a forest by crawling on his stomach and using his crutches as grapnels. He blindly thrusts his crutches into the underbrush that lies in his path and, when they are firmly engaged, pulls himself forward. When he has drawn himself up to the point at which they are caught he repeats the process.

We can link Molloy's use of grapnels with the other machines he has employed to bolster his infirm body and aid him in his locomotion — a bicycle, then crutches (used as such). A pattern emerges: the machines Molloy has used have become progressively simpler and less efficient, requiring an ever greater expenditure of energy on his part. The Cartesian ideal of the perfect man-machine, suggested initially by the bicycle, has been shattered. Man's body degenerates and withers away, ultimately leaving behind a voice. And the machines in which he places his trust and his optimism will be discarded and then crumble away.

Two more patterns must be considered when we treat Molloy's movement. It too has degenerated, having become slower, more painful, and more erratic. First, we can note in Molloy's thrashing through the underbrush his failure to impose order and direction upon his movement by making it conform to a regular geometric figure. Secondly, Molloy is succumbing to entropy. Having begun his journey as a well-ordered system, Molloy, despite the increasing amounts of energy he must put into the system to hold it together, goes over into disorder. The grapnel stage of his

---

[7] Neal Oxenhandler, "The Metaphor of a Metaphor in *La Nausée*," *Chicago Review* 15 (Summer-Autumn 1962), 54.

journey is the last phase of this development before physical motion ceases altogether. Life-in-time, the voyage Molloy is compelled to undertake, is a futile struggle against
increasing chaos and finally yields to inertia. To these patterns we may add still another. Molloy has abandoned the
upright position — particular to the human species. In
creeping along the forest floor like a reptile he has chosen
a means of locomotion that is close to resting and has ac-
knowledged the dehumanization effected by the voyage.

Finally, Molloy's grapnel motion must be situated within
a larger framework of reference — the quest for self. Molloy
is aware that the self he wishes to bring into being is a
timeless and spaceless void from which all movement is
absent. In order to approach this void, Molloy must first
die to external reality by terminating his voyage. However,
the cessation of movement in the macrocosm will be compensated for by verbal movement in the microcosm. And
that movement will generate fiction as it prevents Molloy
from falling silent.

Since this study of the trilogy is intended for an En-
glish-language audience, I shall quote from Beckett's
English translations. *Molloy,* of course, was translated by
Patrick Bowles in collaboration with the author. However,
since Mr. Bowles himself has lauded the "extraordinary
care and concern which Beckett devoted to the work," [8] we
can assume that the translation of *Molloy* is no less author-
itative than the translations of the succeeding volumes of
the trilogy, on which Beckett worked alone.

A systematic comparison of Beckett's translations with
the French originals would doubtlessly offer us new insights
into the workings of Beckett's imagination and increase
our understanding of the trilogy. Not only do Beckett's
translations reveal his extraordinary ability to find linguistic and meta-linguistic equivalents in another language but
they are creative as well, involving changes of meaning and
tone that transcend the exigencies of the disinterested trans-

---

[8] Quoted by Ruby Cohn, *Samuel Beckett: The Comic Gamut* (New
Brunswick, New Jersey: Rutgers University Press, 1962), p. 272.

lator. Such a study would be an ideal subject for a second-generation critic. But until he appears, any general conclusions concerning these diverse modifications must remain highly speculative.

Working within the framework of these limitations and recognizing the number of Beckett's readers who are familiar with the French texts, I have indicated in the notes those places where there are significant departures from the original French that are germane to an analysis of the trilogy's imagery and I have attempted, whenever possible, to explain their purpose or effect.

Chapter I

THE SHRINKING SPACE

I

THERE ARE TWO KINDS OF SPACES. One is the "objective" space of the scientist and the mathematician, depicted in measurements, topological maps, and equations. The other, the kind that concerns us here, is the "living" space that corresponds to a certain human reality and is described not by numbers but by the values accorded to its particular configurations by the individual located in fact or in imagination within one of them. The security of a house; the oppressive confines of a small room in which the self is constricted and turned inward; the limitlessness of sky or ocean into which the self can expand, these are but a few of the possible relationships between an individual and his spatial situation. The space in which an individual operates and his reaction to it can, therefore, reveal a great deal about him. Thus an examination of the respective spatial orientations of the characters of the trilogy will permit us to comprehend more easily the way in which they view the world and function within it.

One thing might appear evident: human existence is spatially structured; we think and act in terms of boundaries, enclosures, dimensions, and distances. However, to discuss, in Frederick Hoffman's terminology, the "spatial circumstances" [1] of the trilogy's protagonists only in terms

---

[1] Frederick J. Hoffman, *Samuel Beckett: The Language of Self* (Carbondale, Illinois: Southern Illinois University Press, 1962), p. 53.

of the spaces one encounters in the course of daily life is not sufficient. The inner space of the protagonist, the space of his mind and his self must be studied as well, for Beckett's particular conception of these entities transforms the notion of existence as space-bound into an absurd paradox from which there is no escape.

II

A voice within Molloy describes the nature of his inner space. That this voice is qualified as a "far whisper" (40) suggests that this space is situated at the deepest level of Molloy's mind or consciousness. It is made up of what are perhaps the entities of the outside world divested of all form and order: "And the thing in ruins. I don't know what it is, what it was, nor whether it was not less a question of ruins than the indestructible chaos of timeless things..." (39). These "ruins" constitute a "place with neither plan nor bounds" (39). But although Molloy calls this space a "place," the word has lost its meaning here because a true place would have an outer limit and a particular configuration that would circumscribe it and differentiate it from other places. Therefore the "place" described by the voice is a somewhere that is aspatial.

Spaceless and timeless as well, for there can be no time in a world where everything is continuously collapsing as if under a great load, but there is none, where nothing changes, begins, or ends: "... these leaning things, forever lapsing and crumbling away, beneath a sky without memory of morning or hope of night" (40). It is a world "at an end" (40), its termination occasioned by its beginning in a continuous process that has abolished past and future and created an atemporal present moment of infinite duration. And where there is no time and space, there can be no true motion. Molloy's inner space is a void, a nothingness beyond or outside space and time-bound reality.

Although Molloy cannot enter his "ruins" at will, when, by chance, he finds himself there, he enjoys an ideal refuge from the outside world: "And I too am at an end, when I am there, my sufferings cease and I end ..." (40). Within this inner realm Molloy is no longer separated from his self, reflecting consciousness and reflected consciousness coincide: "[I] but see and am seen ..." (40). As for Molloy's own dimensions, they have shrunk to nothing: "I wither as the living cannot" (40). "Withering" denotes an indescribable contraction and curling of an object about itself. [2] Selfhood for Molloy thus signifies a liberation from time and space, depicted as a transformation into a dimensionless point in the void. At this juncture, Molloy does not pose the obvious question. How is he to enter a void that has no limits to set it apart from the space-bound existence in which he continues to function? Instead, he stops listening to the voice because, it would seem, he is afraid of the void, even though attaining it, if he could, would terminate his quest for the self.

Moran, on the other hand, has ready access to his mind, entering and leaving it at will, as if there were some sort of boundary or limit that differentiated it from the outside world. And the topography of his mind differs considerably from that of Molloy's. Amid the confusion of preparing to depart on his mission to find Molloy, he pauses for a moment and goes up to his room. There, stretched out on his bed, he meditates: "I wandered in my mind, slowly, noting every detail of the labyrinth, its paths as familiar as those of my garden and yet ever new, as empty as the heart could wish or alive with strange encounters" (106). Although this labyrinthine inner landscape is constantly changing, it does have a comfortable air of familiarity; to use Molloy's term, Moran's mind has a "plan." Whereas Molloy's mind contains no recognizable

---

[2] "Withered" has been substituted for the French "ployé" (59), usually translated as "bent under." The latter is more consonant with the image of the "load" that has supposedly caused the material of Molloy's inner space to collapse. The image of the self that emerges from the French text is that of something that has been reduced to infinitely small dimensions as the result of compression rather than of drying and shriveling.

forms, Moran's is strewn with huge rock-like formations, although he is as ignorant of their nature as Molloy was of the nature of the materials he found in his own inner space.

It is within this region of "finality without end," where things are "massive" and move slowly over time-worn paths, that Moran locates Molloy: "All is dark, but with that simple darkness that follows like a balm upon the great dismemberings. From their places masses move.... Masses of what? One does not ask. There somewhere man is too, vast conglomerate of all of nature's kingdoms.... And in that bloc ... the prey is lodged" (110). The inner region that he describes appears to be situated somewhere between external reality and Molloy's void.

The structures of Moran's inner world have not collapsed, yet some sort of shifting and splitting appears to have already taken place; they seem poised in an equilibrium that is only temporary. Similarly, time and movement have not yet ceased to function, although both seem to have slowed down. Moran is able to locate his "prey" Molloy, but his quest posits the existence of still another level, where the "real" Molloy is to be found: "And the Molloy that I brought to light that memorable August Sunday was certainly not the true denizen of my dark places, for it was not his hour" (114).

Moran's mind does not afford him a total escape from the contingencies of existence, but it does serve as a refuge from the outside world, a world in which Moran sees himself functioning primarily as a body, for it is on his body that the world rains its innumerable and chaotic sense impressions. When he strolls across his inner landscape, he is "far from the world, its clamours, frenzies, bitterness and dingy light" (110). And when he returns to the outside world, he is overwhelmed by the phenomena with which it bombards his senses: "The blood drains from my head, the noise of things bursting, merging, avoiding one another, assails me on all sides, my eyes search in vain for two things alike, each pinpoint of skin screams a different message, I drown in the spray of phenomena. It is at the mercy of these sensations, which happily I know to be illusory, that I have to live and work. It is thanks to them I find myself a meaning" (111).

This opposition between mind and body recalls the Cartesian dualism that appears so frequently in Beckett's works. In his *Sixth Meditation,* Descartes describes the deceptive nature of sensory experience and concludes that "it is the business of the mind alone, and not of the being composed of mind and body, to decide the truth."[3] Although Moran would agree with Descartes, he nonetheless chooses to operate in the outside world. He is ready to dismiss the Molloy he harbors within his mind as a "chimera" and the "weakness of a solitary" (114) and attempts to turn his attention toward the external landscape, where he thinks he will find the less disturbing Molloy "of flesh and blood" (115).

When, later in his quest, Moran meditates upon his identity, he finds that he has changed since his departure: "And on myself too I pored, on me so changed from what I was. And I seemed to see myself ageing as swiftly as a day-fly. And what I saw was more like a crumbling, a frenzied collapsing of all that had always protected me from what I was condemned to be. Or it was like a kind of clawing toward a light and countenance I could not name, that I had once known and long denied. But what words can describe this sensation at first all darkness and bulk, with a noise like the grinding of stones, then suddenly as soft as water flowing" (148). Out of the waters of Moran's inner depths, revealed by the crumbling that has taken place, there floats a face that is recognizably human but that Moran cannot identify, even as to its sex.

The words "darkness," "bulk," and "grinding of stones" leave no doubt that an excavation of sorts has taken place, changing the topography of Moran's mind. We may interpret what has taken place as the collapse of the rocky

---

[3] René Descartes, *The Meditations Concerning First Philosophy,* in *Discourse on Method and Meditations,* trans. Laurence Lafleur (New York: The Library of Liberal Arts, 1964), p. 136.

stratum of everyday existence that formed the upper level of Moran's mind, the level closest to external reality, and in whose categories Moran had frozen his concept of Molloy. The deeper level of Moran's mind that has now been uncovered is no doubt the "dark places" of which he spoke, the level on which not only the real Molloy is to be found, but one on which there will be an endless collapsing as in Molloy's inner void. According to Moran, he and Molloy share the same space, "where Molloy could not be, nor Moran either" (111). The common space, if one can call it a space, that they share is the void where Molloy truly *is*, where Moran would coincide with Molloy: "withered," at one with himself, his mission fulfilled.

Moran is a homeowner, the sort of man who sits in his garden on Sundays reading the Bible and delighting in the domestic sounds all around him. The changes in his relationship to the house reflect the transformations he undergoes during his quest. On the evening of his departure, he finds that his house is partly responsible for his inability to concentrate on his mission: "Finding my spirits as low in the garden as in the house, I turned to go in, saying to myself it was one of two things, either my house had nothing to do with the kind of nothingness in the midst of which I stumbled or else the whole of my property was to blame. To adopt this latter hypothesis was to condone what I had done and in advance what I was to do, pending my departure" (123). Moran's attitude toward leaving his house is ambivalent: on the one hand, he states that he is "happy at heart" (125) to abandon it; on the other, when he is actually on the point of departing, his feelings about leaving his house seem to change. As he turns around to take a final look at his house, the bells of the parish church ring out the hour. But their sound is now meaningless to Moran, who sadly notes: "It did not matter. I was gone from home" (130).

Moran incarnates the man with roots, whereas Molloy, his antithetical self, is, as we see him in the first part of the novel, a vagabond looking for a room in a city whose name he has forgotten. According to Gaston Bachelard, a house functions as an "instrument for braving the cosmos."[4] For Moran it represents the secure and protected existence to which he clings and acts as a barrier that he employs to repress the Molloy element within him. At the same time, however, Moran is relieved to be vacating his house, for he realizes that it symbolizes a mode of existence that is superficial and specious. Fear, guilt, and the happiness of possible liberation give way to resignation and regret when Moran pauses to take a last look at his house before beginning his journey. The comfortable life of a homeowner, whose passing hours were marked by the familiar ringing of the church bells, begins to recede into the past.

But even as he travels toward Molloy country, Moran is not completely "gone from home." He has taken with him his enormous key-ring: "I have a huge bunch of keys, it weighs over a pound. Not a door, not a drawer in my house but the key to it goes with me, wherever I go" (126). His keys represent a continuing link with his house and the type of existence its possession symbolizes. And when, during his struggle with the hulking stranger, the key-ring is broken and the keys scattered on the ground, he employs two unusual methods of retrieving them: he grasps a tuft of grass in each hand and pulls himself from one key to another or, at times, rolls like a cylinder from key to key. He does not find all his keys but "hell to it" he says to himself, "I'll do with those I have" (153).

The stranger with whom Moran grapples and whom he eventually kills greatly resembles Moran. His death suggests a symbolic suicide, the dying of Moran's former self and the unrelenting emergence of the Molloy element within Moran. Molloy's presence is revealed by the methods Moran utilizes to recover his keys, for they closely parallel two means of locomotion that appear in Molloy's narration: the use of his crutches as grapnels to pull himself along the forest floor and his dream of being able to roll like a cylin-

---

[4] Gaston Bachelard, *La Poétique de l'espace*, 4th ed. (Paris: Presses Universitaires de France, 1964), p. 58.

der across the plain that separates the forest from his
mother's room. Moran's keys now constitute a meaningless
insignia for their owner, who does not care if some of them
are missing. Thus, ironically, it is when Moran gathers up
his keys that he imitates the vagabond whose existence he
had sought to repress.

Small wonder, then, that Moran returns as a stranger
to a dark and forbidding house. He does not bother to
check if one of his keys will open the door to his house
and forces his way into the now dark and deserted dwell-
ing. His return, moreover, is only temporary, for, despite
his efforts, he has become indifferent to his house and now
spends most of his time in the garden. He will soon take
up his crutches and voyage once more in search of Molloy.
Living outdoors in the garden, he seems to be preparing
himself for the future hardships he will have to endure.

If Moran is to continue the search for Molloy, his expulsion will be definitive. As he writes his report, he wonders if "the memory of this work brought scrupulously to a
close will help [him] to endure the long anguish of vagran-
cy and freedom." "Does this mean," Moran asks himself, "I
shall one day be banished from my house..." (132)? In
the context of what has already taken place, Moran's question is rhetorical. Gaber's arrival on that peaceful Sunday
afternoon to transmit Youdi's message made his "banish-
ment" inevitable.

The significance of Moran's expulsion from his house
can be extended to Moran *fils*. Moran's departure to search
for Molloy causes his young son to be expelled from his
"pre-pubic paradise,"[5] the safety and protection of his father's house. Youdi orders Moran to take his son with him,
but the boy is reluctant to leave and makes several futile
attempts to remain behind. Moran *fils* is forced to leave at
home his teddy bear and the lamp kept burning at his bed-
side during the night so he will not be afraid of the dark.

---

[5] David Hayman, "Molloy or the Quest for Meaninglessness," in
Samuel Beckett Now, ed. Melvin J. Friedman (Chicago: University
of Chicago Press, 1970), p. 144.

During the course of the journey, the young Moran first aids his father and then abandons him, thereby asserting his own independence. Although he eventually returns to his father's house, the relationship between father and son has been irrevocably altered. Moran *fils* is no longer a little boy dependent upon his father. He has been initiated into the real world, where there are no teddy bears and no nightlights to protect him from the dark.

Molloy does not, of course, possess a house; but he does have a room, his mother's room, the goal of his journey and its terminus. Mag, his mother, is not there when he arrives, so he cannot question her about his existence (for which he holds her responsible) — its justification or its meaning. Nonetheless it is by means of the room that Molloy finds her anew, and the space of the room becomes analogous to the womb: "I have her room. I sleep in her bed. I piss and shit in her pot. I have taken her place" (7). Molloy had always considered the time spent within the warm, protective space of his mother's womb as the only "endurable" (18) period of his life.

Molloy's symbolic return to the womb suggests both death and rebirth. Death not in the physical sense of the word — Molloy is not sure whether he is dead or alive — but in the sense that he is now very close to being dead to the outside world. His *Wanderjahre* are now terminated, and the walls of the room separate him from external reality. Perhaps, having returned to where his life began, he can now find a birth more satisfactory than the traumatic experience that expelled him from the womb and thrust him into a world he did not choose. Now that he has replaced his mother, he must somehow give birth to himself. Until he can find a means of accomplishing that feat, Molloy must remain in exile, even in the womb substitute he has found, and his voyage continues: "But now I do not wander any more, anywhere any more, and indeed I scarcely stir at all, and yet nothing is changed. And the confines of my room, of my bed, of my body, are as remote from me as were those of my region, in the days of my splendour. And the cycle continues, joltingly, of flight and bivouac, in

an Egypt without bounds, without infant, without mother"
(66). Molloy remains lost in darkest Egypt, the land of
exile for the Israelites and, according to the Gospel of Saint
Matthew, for Joseph, Mary, and the Infant Jesus fleeing
from the wrath of Herod.

In order to be reborn and end his exile from the self,
Molloy must become a dimensionless point in the void. His
portrayal of the "confines" of his room, bed, and body
bring us back to the question of how Molloy was to enter
his inner void if there was no way of circumscribing it.
Molloy passes from the larger space of his room to the
smaller space of his body as if he were trying to delimit
his self, detaching it from the overlapping spaces that
envelop it. However, Molloy is attempting to bring together
two distinct realms: a spaceless self and various spatial
configurations. Given the incommensurability of the two, he
cannot establish a frontier between them. And relatively
speaking, if we think of the self as an infinitely small point,
the spaces that Molloy mentions are immense when compared to it. Thus even within the limited confines of his
mother's room, Molloy can be as far away from his goal
as he ever was.

The incommensurability between the space of the mind
and that of the body suggests another influence of Cartesian
dualism. Using the spatiality of the body as his point of
departure, spatial extension was the first attribute that
Descartes assigned to the material world. But if man's essence, according to Descartes, is that he thinks, then his
essential self must be aspatial, for the mind is pure spirit:
". . . since on the one hand I have a clear and distinct idea
of myself in so far as I am only a thinking and not an extended being, and since on the other hand I have a distinct
idea of body, in so far as it is only an extended being which
does not think it is certain that this I (that is to say, my
soul by virtue of which I am what I am) is entirely (and
truly) distinct from my body. . . ." [6] Consequently, the body

---

[6] Descartes, *Meditations on First Philosophy*, p. 152.

is but the container for the mind. The space of that container can be reduced by loss of limbs or mutilation and the self brought closer. Thus during his voyage Molloy loses his toes.

Age and degeneration have caused Molloy to become increasingly abstracted from external reality. As his relationships with it have diminished, his consciousness has become more purified and selfhood brought closer to realization. Molloy's essential link with reality is now the words that he uses in his narration. Thus his mother's room becomes the mental microcosm from which his tale emanates. Within it Molloy's journey continues linguistically, for it is by means of his narration that he recreates the world outside his room as he attempts to seize his identity by relating the events that brought him to where he is.

But Molloy only knows "what the words know" (31). And what do they know? They describe a space-bound world, one that Molloy has rejected. But can the words describe a nothingness, a "place" that is not a place, a self that is dimensionless? That they cannot establishes one of the crucial problems of the trilogy. Obliged to write as a means of self-discovery, Molloy is forced to use words that are unable to describe, and thus bring into being, his true self. They are the heritage of a long process of evolution over which Molloy had no control and, ultimately, they constitute a foreign language. Lacking the necessary language of self, Molloy creates fiction when he attempts to tell his own story and finally fall silent. Writing thus becomes an absurd and futile task, one without end: "And truly it little matters what I say, this, this or that or any other thing. Saying is inventing. Wrong, very rightly wrong. You invent nothing, you think you are inventing, you think you are escaping, and all you do is stammer out your lesson, the remnants of a pensum one day got by heart and long forgotten, life without tears, as it is wept. To hell with it anyway" (31-32).

Moran's room is potentially the same as Molloy's. When Moran retreats to his room to meditate, it becomes the space of "Being enclosed," [7] a shelter that separates Moran from the outside world and turns him inward toward the self. "Lying down, in the warmth, in the gloom" (110), Moran has but a narrow threshold to cross in order to enter his mind. Moran's room suggests a womb, though the analogy is plainly less developed than in the case of Molloy. Although Moran writes his report in his room, the latter is not the terminus of his existence. The outside world is still very much of a real entity for Moran, who faces the prospect of a long voyage in his continuing search for Molloy. Given these similarities, we may assume that when Moran's vagabondage is over, he will face an exile no different from Molloy's.

Beckett leaves little doubt that Moran will spend that time writing. The report that Moran drafts for Youdi is not his first. The subjects of Moran's past reports reveal him to be the creator of Beckett's other novels: "Oh the stories I could tell you, if I were easy. What a rabble in my head, what a gallery of moribunds. Murphy, Watt, Yerk, Mercier and all the others. I would never have believed that — yes I believe it willingly. Stories, stories. I have not been able to tell them. I shall not be able to tell this one" (137). [8] Moran's past efforts at creation have been a failure. None of the characters he names, however, seem to have brought about the sort of disturbance in Moran's existence that Molloy does; nor did any of them constitute an antithetical self that Moran had tried to repress. Moran is in the process of discovering that the object of the writer is the capture of his own elusive essence. In order to seize it, Moran must free himself from the chains of his bourgeois existence and become the one whom he seeks to bring into existence. Edith Kern compares Moran's mission to the "task which Yeats had set for each man, and the poet in particular: to

---

[7] Ludovic Janvier, *Pour Samuel Beckett* (Paris: Editions de Minuit, 1966), p. 51.

[8] Yerk does not appear in any of Beckett's known works. John Fletcher relates that Beckett told him he does not know who Yerk is either. See *The Novels of Samuel Beckett* (London: Chatto and Windus, 1964), pp. 156-157.

seek out the 'other self, the antiself or the antithetical self' and, indeed, to become — 'of all things not impossible the most difficult' — that other self." [9]

While Molloy is traveling toward his mother's room, he finds substitutes for it in the temporary shelters in which he takes refuge. Analogous to the room, they limit his space, reducing it from the larger spaces through which he voyages to a small enclosure that circumscribes Molloy and draws him closer to his self. In addition, of course, they offer him protection from the elements and from the hostility of his fellow men.

The first of these shelters is located in the city where Lousse saves Molloy after he runs over her dog. It is a "narrow alley between two buildings" (60) on to which face the bathroom windows. The passageway is actually a cul-de-sac, at the end of which is a wall with two alcoves piled with garbage, old newspapers, and dog droppings. And it is in one of these alcoves — Molloy, ironically, refers to them as "chapels" — that he thinks of taking refuge: "For the space of an instant, I considered settling down there, making it my lair and sanctuary, for the space of an instant" (61). Molloy, the jetsam of humanity, finds himself perfectly at home amid the detritus of existence. He even makes a half-hearted gesture at suicide, as if "chapel" and death could truly replace his mother's room and the possibility of rebirth that lies therein. Despite the temporary respite his shelter affords, he must abandon it.

Some time later, we find Molloy in a cavern by the seashore: "And in the morning, in my cave, and even sometimes at night, when the storm raged, I felt reasonably secure from the elements and mankind. But there too there is a price to pay. In your box, in your caves, there too there is a price to pay. And which you pay willingly, for a time, but you cannot go on paying forever" (75). Molloy extends the image of the room substitute by comparing the cave to his "box" — the Cartesian notion of man as a thinking

---

[9] Edith Kern, "Moran-Molloy: The Author as Hero," *Perspective*, 11 (Autumn 1959), 186.

container. Both "chapel" and cave form a sort of second "box," one that fits closely around the first (i.e., the body) and provides a more effective barrier against external reality. But time, Molloy realizes, is the price he must pay for these pauses in his journey. Time is passing, and Molloy must penetrate beyond his "box" if he is to bring time and space to an end.

Unlike Molloy, who finds his shelters by chance, Moran, during the early stages of his journey, constructs his own shelters out of branches. For Moran they serve as substitutes for both his room and his house. In the first instance they enable Moran to duplicate the conditions of darkness, immobility, and encompassment that he enjoyed in his room and which permitted him to enter the recesses of his consciousness. Thus he withdraws to his shelter to think about his mission: "Stretched out in the shelter, I brooded on the undertaking in which I was embarked. I tried again to remember what I was to do with Molloy, when I found him" (145). In the second instance, and despite Moran's ambiguous happiness about leaving his house, they serve as a substitute house, an oasis of order and safety in the midst of the radical transformation that Moran's life is undergoing. When Moran explores his camp site, his movements describe a star-like configuration in which the shelter becomes a center of security: "... I kept my eye on the shelter, which drew me with an extraordinary pull, so that to cut across the terminus of one sally to the terminus of the next and so on, which would have been convenient, was out of the question. But each time I had to retrace my steps, the way I had come to the shelter, and make sure all was in order before I sallied forth again" (148).

For part of his journey Moran must share his shelters with his son. Although he continues to treat his son in his usual tyrannical fashion, within the shelters they share, Moran's breath "mingles" (160) with that of his son, creating an intimacy in their relationship that did not exist prior to Moran's departure from his house. After his son abandons him, Moran's contradictory feelings about the boy are manifested by his reluctance to build shelters. They would compel him to think about his son, whose presence is represented by the forced and transparent image of the trench coat he used to wear: "But I did not like proper shelters, made of boughs, any more. For soon there were no more leaves, but only the needles of certain conifers. But this was not the real reason why I did not like proper shelters any more, no. But when I was inside them I could think of nothing but my son's raincoat, I literally saw it, I saw nothing else, it filled all space" (172). On the one hand, Moran is ready to admit that his reluctance to build shelters was due to his son's disappearance; on the other, he refuses to acknowledge that he truly missed his son by substituting the raincoat for his son's body. Whatever the reason for Moran's disinclination to build shelters, his dependence on those he finds by chance on the way home — hedges, tree trunks, etc. — testifies to the transformation of his existence during his mission and reinforces his growing resemblance to Molloy.

Both Molloy and Moran wished to be confined within the narrow space of a room. While at the seashore Molloy exhibits an opposing tendency, one we do not find in Moran. Molloy enjoys the contemplation of vast, unbroken spaces. [10] By situating his relatively small body within much larger spaces, Molloy is able to reduce himself to a "black speck in the great pale stretch of sand" (74). Although he seems unaware of it, his shrinking to a seemingly dimensionless point in the void-like emptiness of the sand constitutes an analogue of the description of his self by his inner voice. A similar obliteration of his person is revealed by his recollection of a sea voyage made perhaps during a previous sojourn at the shore: "And I too once went forth on it, in a sort of oarless skiff, but I paddled with an old bit of driftwood. And I sometimes wonder if I ever came back from that voyage. For if I see myself putting to sea, and the long hours without landfall, I do not see the return..."

---

[10] Ludovic Janvier notes this "tendance au large" in the protagonists of the *Stories. Pour Samuel Beckett*, p. 51.

(69). His inability to recall his return suggests a present desire on his part to be reduced to the minute and almost nonexistent figure of a man in a small boat adrift on the limitless expanse of the sea.

These two images of the point in the void are reinforced by the improvement in Molloy's eyesight during this period. Before coming to the seashore, Molloy was unable to differentiate himself, the observer, from what he observed: "And of my two eyes only one functioning more or less correctly, I misjudged the distance separating me from the other world, and often I stretched out my hand for what was far beyond my reach and often I knocked against obstacles scarcely visible on the horizon" (50). Now with vast expanses of beach on three sides and the ocean before him, he discovers that he sees better: "Let me tell you something, my sight was better at the seaside! Yes, ranging far and wide over these vast flats, where nothing lay, nothing stood, my good eye saw more clearly and there were even days when the bad one too had to look away" (75). Molloy's problem is not with his eyes but with his inability to separate his consciousness from what it contemplates. As we saw in Molloy's localization of himself within his mother's room, he must establish some sort of boundary between the spacelessness of his mind and the space of external reality in order to enter the void. Away from the beach, he was unable to establish a line of demarcation between himself and the outside world — the "other world." At the seashore, the problem no longer exists: observer and observed, the dimensionless point that Molloy has become and the unbroken reaches of sand and ocean that give the impression of being immeasurably vast, and hence dimensionless, merge into one. Thus the particular topography of the seashore is able to furnish Molloy with a temporary and limited freedom from the bounds of spatiality.

Another aspect of the problem of the incommensurability of space-bound existence and the spaceless self is presented by Molloy's depiction of his region. He states that he has never been able to travel far from his native city:

"And yet I knew the town well, for I was born there and had never succeeded putting between it and me more than ten or fifteen miles, such was its grasp on me..." (31). If, as he tells us, he has never been in any other city but his own, then the two seemingly different cities he enters during the course of his wandering can be interpreted as different aspects of the same city, Molloy's voyage, then, consists of going in and out of his city and traveling through the nearby countryside. This first region described by Molloy's movements is not only limited by the proximity of its borders to the city where his mother's room is located but also by the coastline of the island that Molloy inhabits: "And that my land went no further, in one direction at least, did not displease me" (68). Yet despite its apparent smallness, we discover that Molloy's region is, paradoxically, indeterminately large: "...Molloy, your region is vast, you have never left it and you never shall. And wheresoever you wander, within its distant limits, things will always be the same, precisely" (65-66). Moreover, in seeming contradiction to what he said about the shores of his island, Molloy claims that his region does not stop there: "But don't imagine my region ended at the coast, that would be a grave mistake. For it was this sea too, its reefs and distant islands, and its hidden depths" (69).

Obviously, Molloy is confusing — in the literal sense of the word — two different regions. The first is the territory he covers during his travels, the region of external reality, measurable in miles and delimited by borders. The second, the larger region that includes the first and stretches far beyond its limits, can be termed the region of the self. Analogous to the relative immensity of Molloy's room when compared to his self, the space of Molloy's voyage is similarly vast and might just as well include the entire earth. Whatever limits Molloy might assign to the region through which he wanders, his self will be as far from them as it was from the walls of his room.

Moran's depiction of Molloy's region differs markedly from the way in which Molloy described it. And this disparity reflects the differences in modes of existence between

the two protagonists as well as the changes Moran undergoes during his quest. His initial localization of Molloy
within a carefully delimited area is a means of identifying
his quarry and recalls his having petrified him in the conceptions and logic of everyday existence. Thus Moran, unlike
Molloy himself, knows the name of Molloy's native city,
Bally. He is also familiar with the divisions of Molloy's
region: "In modern countries this is what I think is called
a commune, or a canton ... but there exists with us no
abstract and generic term for such territorial subdivisions.
And to express them we have another system, of singular
beauty and simplicity, which consists in saying Bally ...
when you mean Bally and Ballyba when you mean Bally
plus its domains and Ballybaba when you mean the domains exclusive of Bally itself" (133-134). As for the size of
Molloy's regions, Moran assigns it a "surface area of five
or six square miles at the most" and notes that Molloy
has never crossed its "administrative limits" (133).

    With all his knowledge of Molloy's region, Moran arrives
in Ballyba "without knowing it" (158). And after failing to
reach Bally, he wonders if his information had been correct: "That then is a part of what I thought about Ballyba
when I left home. I wonder if I was not confusing it with
some other place" (135). Moran's doubt reflects back upon
his own place of residence. He hesitates as to whether or
not he still lives in "Turdy, hub of Turdyba" (134). The
dislocation that occurs in Moran's geography is not only
an indication of his inability to seize Molloy but also, in a
more general sense, an erosion of his ability to structure his
existence with the tools of logic and order. And Moran's
hesitation with regard to his own region reveals a further
blurring of the separation between himself and Molloy.
Although Moran is unaware of their humor, the names
that Beckett assigns to the regions of his two protagonists
reinforce the absurdity of Moran's efforts at situating himself and Molloy. The connotations of Turdy need no com-
ment. As for Bally, it may suggest, as William York Tindall
has pointed out, a corruption of Baile atha Cliath, the

Gaelic name for Dublin.[11] More likely, however, the name is based on the colloquial word for testicles. The addition of the suffix "baba" to these names, syllables that sound like the bleating of sheep, further underlines the meaninglessness of the exterior landscape, such as Moran attempts to delineate it.

We can see, then, how in both narrations the notion of space breaks down and how each protagonist's journey is two-fold: the voyage through the space of external reality parallels the voyage toward the self. If we consider the two narrations simultaneously, then Molloy is retreating as Moran pursues him. Yet if as Moran states, he cannot be where Molloy is not, then their spaces must merge. But this can only take place in the spacelessness of the self, outside language and outside the novel.

III

Like his predecessors, Malone, dying in his room, is also a writer. More importantly, he resembles Moran in that he identifies himself as the creator of Beckett's other novels. Recalling the writing of *Molloy*, he repeats several lines from the beginning of that novel and then expresses his discontent with what he has produced: "I have often amused myself with trying to invent them [the events of *Molloy*].... But without succeeding in amusing myself really" (183). Malone now hopes that his death will put an end to his writing career: "Then it will be over with the Murphys, Merciers, Molloys, Morans and Malones, unless it goes on beyond the grave" (236). Malone's inclusion of himself among his fictions reveals a clear awareness of the disparity between his real self and the characters he creates. He has never succeeded in relating his own story, never succeeded in coinciding with one of his protagonists. Now Malone decides that the stories he will tell will

---

[11] William York Tindall, *Samuel Beckett* (New York and London: Columbia University Press, 1964), p. 24.

constitute a simple diversion, a means of passing away the time. Instead of being implicated in his stories, he will be "neutral and inert" (179). But he soon discovers that the two characters he creates, Saposcat, nicknamed Sapo (whom other people think a sap) and Macmann (son of man), are but two aspects of himself: Malone as a young man and Malone as an old man. "I wonder," Malone states, "if I am not talking yet again about myself. Shall I be incapable to the end of lying on any other subject?" (189). Malone is therefore compelled to resign himself to the fact that writing is not an innocent pastime but a means of self-discovery: "I did not want to write, but I had to resign myself to it in the end. It is in order to know where I have got to, where he [Sapo] has got to" (207).

"Live and invent" (194), Malone asserts. The writer lives through his fictions, but his life is therefore an invention. As Dina Dreyfus puts it: "Entirely estranged in his fictions, the novelist is neither able to recognize himself in them, nor seize his own reality outside them, nor coincide with the stories he invents, nor create, without inventing it, his own story." [12] Hence Saposcat and Macmann become, to use Richard Coe's apt term, "pseudo-personalities" [13] of the author (for Malone they are "homuncules" [225]). Moreover, as we have seen, Malone is ultimately no less a fiction than his pseudo-personalities, though as the narrator of the stories he has a special status.

If to invent is to live, then to write is to be trapped in time, in the sense that Malone's stories pass the time, reduce the time remaining to Malone before he dies. Their fabrication takes him beyond his room and simultaneously brings him back to his dying. Malone's stratagem is to annihilate his fictions at the same time that he himself passes away: to eliminate his past and his more recent

[12] Dina Dreyfus, "Vraies et fausses énigmes," *Mercure de France*, 330 (October 1957), 281.

[13] Richard N. Coe, *Samuel Beckett* (New York: Grove Press, 1964), p. 64.

past and, at the moment of death, to permit his silent self to be born, to attain the "blessedness of absence" (222).

This simultaneity of dying and creating fictions, of being inside the room and outside it, is conveyed by imagery of shrinking and expansion. Malone also considers his self to be a dimensionless point and, analogous to Molloy's "withering," he describes a process of diminution during which he becomes so "hard and contracted" that he "would be lost in the eye of a needle" (225). Malone thought that as he died this shrinking would continue until he became a dimensionless point. But he discovers that he cannot accomplish this without a corresponding expansion, a departure from the self through the creation of fiction: "All the stories I have told myself ... swelling, swelling" (225). Hence as Malone "withers" his body becomes immense: his feet are so far away that they are "beyond the range of the most powerful telescope" (234); if he were to defecate, the "lumps would fall out in Australia"; and if he were to stand up he would fill "a considerable part of the universe" (235). [14]

The room plays an important role both in Macmann's story and in Malone's dying. Macmann's cruel and painful existence in the macrocosm, exemplified by a pelting rain that tortures Macmann as he lies in a cruciform position in the middle of a field, is rejected for the ataraxia of a confinement in a womb-like room: ".... a place impermeable as far as possible to wind, rain, sound, cold, great heat ... and daylight" (245). Macmann, however, never attains this degree of quietude. After he is placed in an

---

[14] The imagery of contraction and expansion is more explicit and more extensive in the French text. There, Malone contrasts his gigantic body, swollen by his narration, with the possibility of being "enterré dans un écrin à bijoux presque" (113). The translation attenuates the comparison but gains the humour of "almost buried in a casket" (235). The image of the jewel-box is extended by a somewhat obscure passage excised from the English. In it we find two images of the self as a tiny point, "minuscule tête de lard enfouie quelque part dans ma vraie tête" and "réduit aux dimensions d'une ocelle de noctuelle" as well as another description of Malone's huge body, "l'énormité éparse dans l'ombre" (114).

asylum, he discovers that his room there can only offer
him a frosted window that cannot be opened. But Moll,
Macmann's nurse and mistress, not only polishes the window so that more light will enter but also destroys the
tranquility of the room by introducing within its walls and
into Macmann's life the emotion of love. Macmann is so
disturbed by this new experience, when all he sought was
isolation, that he comes to reject his room: "... he mourn-
ed the long immunity he had lost, from shelter, charity and
human tenderness" (265-266).

Macmann abandons his room at the asylum for a substitute refuge, a "lair" (275) he has dug at the foot of a
bush on the grounds. Whenever he can, Macmann encloses
himself within this protective space that is intermediate
between the room and the space of external reality. Here
too Macmann does not find the peace he desires and so, just
the opposite of Molloy and Moran, he longs to return to the
space of the macrocosm: "... seeking a way out into
the desolation of having nobody and nothing, the wilds
of the hunted, the scant bread and the scant shelters and
the black joy of the solitary way ..." (278).

Malone, of course, is already confined to a room, his
journey in the macrocosm terminated. But the space of
his room is not completely separated from that of the outside world due to the existence of a window beside his
bed. [15] The window represents Malone's continuing relationship with external reality, the reality to which he is in the
process of dying and whose disappearance will mark his
liberation from space. The passage of time has weakened
that relationship; the window is "misted and smeared with
the filth of years" (198). Nonetheless, the world outside the
window is a source of sustenance for Malone because
the stories he relates are projections into that world, projections whose purpose is to permit Malone to be reborn

---

[15] The relationship between the room, the window, and external
reality is more clearly defined in the original. A phrase deleted
from the English depicts Malone's room as "cet endroit encore au
monde mal fermé" (119).

when he dies. Consequently, Malone describes himself as an "old foetus . . . hoar and impotent" (225) and the window through which he derives his nourishment becomes his "umbilicus" (223).

During the course of his narration Malone's room undergoes several modifications, which reveal another aspect of the expansion and contraction that he is undergoing. One of these is the transformation of the room into a skull. Like Molloy and Moran, Malone locates the self in the mental realm. Thus as he approaches it, he sees himself retreating within a head: ". . . it seems to me I am in a head and that these eight, no, six, these six planes that enclose me are of solid bone" (221). Where once he saw flowered paper peeling from the walls of his room, he now sees a "gleaming and shimmering as of bones" (223). His room has become a "foul little den all dirty white and vaulted as though hollowed out of ivory" (236).

Yet it is not enough for Malone to retreat within this skull-room. He must ultimately depart from it. Malone is a fiction, an idea, so to speak, in someone's head. Malone's real self cannot be a fiction because it lies outside the domain of language; it cannot be situated in the skull-room. In order to be reborn Malone must vacate the room, leaving emptiness behind him. Indeed, Malone mistakenly believes he has accomplished this when, having leaned over his bed to pick up something, he thinks he and Sapo have flowed out of his head: ". . . in my head I suppose all was streaming and emptying away as though through a sluice, to my great joy, until finally nothing remained, either of Malone or of the other" (224).

Malone's rebirth, his departure from the room and his liberation from space, is heralded by the metamorphosis of his room into womb, not the static image we found in *Molloy*, but that of a womb in labor: "The ceiling rises and falls, rises and falls, rythmically, as when I was a foetus" (283). Analogous to the breaking of the amniotic sac (and recalling the image of the water-filled skull), a "noise of rushing water" (283) is heard. Finally, Malone's feet begin to clear the "great cunt of existence" (283).

As Malone is reborn his narration grounds to a halt. Lemuel coalesces with Malone after killing off the remaining characters. Just before the concluding negation of time, Malone signals the end of space by noting "never there" (288); "there," the word we use to indicate space, no longer has any reference.

But must Malone die — and his narration cease — in order for his spaceless self to be born? If this is so, then Malone has not solved anything: he has not described that self and hence not brought it into being. According to his own statement, Malone can only live as a fiction, and now he has been annihilated. "Unless it continues beyond the grave," Malone said of his relationship with his fictions. The investigation of that relationship and of the problem of self-knowledge will indeed continue beyond the grave, in the last volume of the trilogy, *The Unnamable*.

IV

The opening words of *The Unnamable*, "Where now?" (291), immediately reveal that the quest for an escape from space-bound existence has not been terminated. However, the very existence of the nameless narrator of the novel is an absurdity. He is the self that his predecessors in the trilogy sought. He is a dimensionless point in the void; but until he finds the words that will say nothing, he cannot locate himself: "Enormous prison, like a hundred thousand cathedrals ... and in it, somewhere, perhaps, riveted, tiny, the prisoner, how can he be found, how false this space is, what falseness, instantly ... to want to put a being there ..." (409). If the Unnamable can describe where he is, he will be able to give himself a name, a name that will coincide with his *I* and not describe a fiction.

It is precisely this falling back into fiction that the Unnamable wishes to avoid in his search for self. Like Moran and Malone before him, the Unnamable identifies himself as the creator of the novels that preceded his; he is the source from which the trilogy springs. Now encircled by the characters he has created, he denounces his works. His search for self-knowledge has hitherto been a failure because it has brought forth only fiction: "All these Murphys, Molloys and Malones do not fool me. They have made me waste my time, suffer for nothing, speak of them, when, in order to stop speaking, I should have spoken of me and of me alone" (303). Now the Unnamable attributes the words he uses to Basil and his cohorts, the "delegates" (297) who furnish the Unnamable with what the words mirror — information about external reality. Obviously, Basil and company, as well as the Unnamable qua narrator, are only fictions. Their existence is perpetuated by the Unnamable's inability to find a language of self.

The first spatial configuration that the Unnamable establishes in his attempt to describe his spatial situation is his "charmed circle" (300). "Fixed at the center" (295) of the circle is the Unnamable, the creator; the circumference of the circle is constituted by the orbit of Malone, his creation. That which we habitually designate as the center of a circle is, in reality, not a spatial entity but a dimensionless point. Thus the center of the circle becomes an image of the Unnamable's spaceless self. He still needs, however, to describe his location. We can also recall here the traditional definition of God as a circle whose center is everywhere and whose circumference is nowhere. God is the indefinable essence of all things, the dimensionless center from which his infinite creation emanates. Just as the center of a circle is the locus of points on or within the circle, the divine presence is manifested in every aspect of his creation, and all these aspects are unified in their creator.

However, Malone is a fiction, whereas the Unnamable is not. As such, Malone can die — as he does at the conclusion of *Malone Dies* — and hence transcend spatiality: "...Malone revolves, a stranger forever to my infirmities, one who is not as I can never not be ... he is the God" (300). If the Unnamable could find the proper words, he would be able to say, I, Malone, and be the Malone he was hitherto unable to become. He could then portray Malone as a dimensionless point, or, what amounts to the same thing, have Malone trace an infinitely large orbit. Like God, the Unnamable would then be circumference and center, the alpha and omega of the world his Word has brought into being. But unable to describe his own aspatiality, he is forced to portray Malone as a spatial entity and have him revolve in a finite orbit. Therefore, the Unnamable cannot be at the center of the circle but must be somewhere between the center and the circumference: "From center to circumference . . . is a far cry," the Unnamable admits, "and I may well be situated between the two" (295).

Thus the Unnamable can perceive himself only at a distance. His search for self posits an "elsewhere" — a fiction — that is not the dimensionless "here," where the Unnamable knows his real self to be located, where he knows he has always been. The Unnamable confesses that there is no one orbiting around him. His "charmed circle" was only a fiction, invented, the Unnamable states, "to put off the hour when I must speak of me" (304). The Unnamable has already demonstrated his inability to speak about himself.

If the Unnamable were to exist in space, he would possess a body; and he accords himself one, provisonally. He portrays himself as seated cross-legged, with tears from his eyes rolling down his face and body. The most salient manifestation of the body's spatiality is its protrusions: hair, facial features, genitals, limbs. Stripped of these elements, the body takes the form of an urn-shaped torso, crowned by a head — Cartesian man as a thinking container. If the container is still further reduced, we are left with a head — the part of the body that encloses the mind — whose essential shape is that of an egg or ball. Within that head, man pursues his essential function — thinking, and hence speaking, for the two according to Beckett are indissociable.

The Unnamable's body undergoes just this sort of reduction. Speaking of his tears, he states: "They gather in my beard and from there, when it can hold no more — no, no beard . . ." (305). This abrupt "no" signals the beginning of the rejection of the Unnamable's body. "All the things that stick out" (305) fall away. The eyes that streamed tears and with which he observed Malone and the lights of the "delegates" also disappear: "I'll dry these streaming sockets, bung them up, there, its done, no more tears ..." (305). Finally, all that is left of the Unnamable is a "big talking ball" (305).

As pure consciousness, the Unnamable cannot have a body. Moreover, his description of himself as a "big talking ball" is false on two accounts. Firstly, we know that the Unnamable is silent. Secondly, the word "big" implies that he has certain dimensions; however, the Unnamable is dimensionless. Consequently, the Unnamable is forced to amend his self-portrait: "I always knew I was round, round and solid ... no apertures, invisible perhaps, or as vast as Sirius in the Great Dog. These expressions mean nothing" (305-306).

The Unnamable's depiction of himself as a perfect sphere parallels his earlier attempt to place himself at the center of a circle. The two figures — circle and sphere — have traditionally been used almost interchangeably as symbols of divinity. *Deus est sphaera cuius centrum ubique, circumferentia nusquam.* The size of the sphere is therefore not measurable in spatial terms. But lacking the words that could portray him as he really is, the Unnamable is obliged to use epithets drawn from space-bound language in his vain attempt to seize the unmeasurable.

When the Unnamable rejects his body, he rejects his eyes as well. Yet their disappearance does not prevent him from describing what he sees. However, in order for something to be seen, there must be an observer and a certain distance between him and that which he observes. If the Unnamable is aspatial, he does not fulfill these conditions. As Robert Champigny has noted with regard to the Unnamable: "That which is seen can be considered as forming part of the look [regard], therefore of the self." [16] This

---

[16] Robert Champigny, "Les Aventures de la première personne," in *Configuration critique de Samuel Beckett,* ed. Melvin J. Friedman

"self" is not, however, the real self of the Unnamable because the "look" does not belong to him. It is therefore
language that determines the existence of the Unnamable
as spectator, that forces him to exist spatially by virtue of
what he sees and describes.

A skull with its limited space and protecting walls is the
antithesis of the Unnamable's "vast prison." As we have
already seen, it is also the microcosm from which fictions
emanate. The Unnamable recalls Malone's skull-room when
he wonders if he could be situated within a skull: "The
inside of my distant skull where once I wandered, now am
fixed, lost for tininess, or straining against the walls . . ."
(303). But Malone's withdrawal into a skull would have no
meaning in the case of the Unnamable because the Unnamable is the self born when Malone's skull was emptied. He
cannot be in a head because he is not a fiction. Moreover,
the disembodied Unnamable could not possess a skull. It
is therefore only fear of never being able to assign himself
a space and the concomitant desire to shed the burden of
achieving selfhood by according himself fictional status that
causes the Unnamable to evoke a now meaningless image:
"And sometimes I say to myself I am in a head. It's terror
makes me say it, and the longing to be in safety, surrounded
on all sides by massive bone" (350).

This same longing to forsake the dilemma of defining
his present space is manifested in the reappearance of other
spaces from the first two volumes of the trilogy. The Unnamable's skill in describing them only exacerbates the
frustration he now feels: "Help, help, if I could only describe this place, I who am so good at describing places"
(399). There is, of course, the room: ". . . if I could put
myself in a room, that would be the end of the wordy-
gurdy . . ." (399). "A cell would be plenty," the Unnamable

(Paris: Minard, 1964), p. 125. For reasons of clarity, I have translated Professor Champigny's French rather than use the English
version of the same article. Cf. "Adventures of the First Person,"
in *Samuel Beckett Now*, p. 123.

laments, "if I gave up, if only I could give up" (409). Even the luxuriant foliage of a forest — recalling Molloy's journey — would be sufficient: "... a roof is not indispensable, if I could be in a forest, caught in a thicket, or wandering around in circles, it would be an end of this blither" (319). Unwilling to transform himself anew into one of his previous incarnations and thus return to these sheltering spaces — to "give up" as the Unnamable puts it — the Unnamable must confront the possibility of eternal exile, "a stranger in [his] own midst, surrounded by invaders" (396). These "invaders" are his "delegates," that is to say, the words foreign to his own reality in which he is forced to perpetuate his contradictory existence — "I am all these words, all these strangers" (386).

There is another avenue that the Unnamable explores in his effort to say where he is. Just as Malone had his "homuncules," the Unnamable has his "vice-existers" (315) — Mahood and Worm. And, paradoxically, despite his previous failures, he seeks a means of coinciding with them. Since the words have usurped his existence, Basil is rechristened Mahood, and it is Mahood who tells his own story (as well as that of Worm) to the Unnamable: "It was he who told me stories about me, lived in my stead, issued forth from me, came back to me, entered back into me, heaped stories on my head" (308).

When his period as a voyager is over, Mahood, minus his one arm and his one leg, comes to rest: "Stuck like a sheaf of flowers in a deep jar, its neck flush with my mouth, on the side of a quiet street near the shambles ..." (327). Analogous to the Unnamable's rejection of his body, whose appendages represented the most evident sign of his spatial extension, Mahood has passed from his former mutilated state to that of being a torso and a head. In losing his remaining limbs, Mahood has only shed more of his spatiality and in the process has come closer to the essential self: "I may therefore perhaps legitimately suppose that the one armed one legged wayfarer of a moment ago and the wedge-headed trunk in which I am now marooned are simply two phases of the same carnal envelope, the soul being notoriously immune from deterioration and dismemberment. Having lost one leg, what indeed more likely than I should mislay the other? And similarly for the arms. A natural transition in sum" (330). And with Mahood in his jar, the process of reduction continues: "I have dwindled, I dwindle. Not so long ago, with a kind of shrink of my head and shoulders, as when one is scolded, I could disappear. Soon, at my present rate of decrease, I may spare myself this effort" (331).

If Mahood is a representation of the Unnamable, how great, we may ask, is the separation between the two? How much more of his body must Mahood lose before he merges with the Unnamable? The latter foresees a series of progressive reductions that would shrink Mahood to a dimensionless point, stripping away his "carnal envelope" until Mahood becomes the essential self — pure "soul": "Mutilate, mutilate, and perhaps some day, fifteen generations hence, you'll succeed in looking like yourself..." (315).

The literature that would result from this project would be, as Hugh Kenner has remarked, an "endgame." [17] Given an infinite number of Mahoods and an endles period of time, or, what amounts to the same thing, an endless series of interlocking novels, the result would always be the same: without a language to describe spacelessness there would remain one last Mahood to separate the Unnamable from himself.

As long as Mahood remains space-bound, there is no possibility that he and the Unnamable can coincide, and his story is abandoned for that of Worm: "The stories of Mahood are ended. He has realized they could not be about me..." (345). As his second vice-exister's name indicates, we have left the world of men — Mahood's world — and descended the ladder of evolution. Worm "having nothing human, has nothing else, has nothing, is nothing" (346).

---

[17] Hugh Kenner, *Samuel Beckett: A Critical Study* (New York: Grove Press, 1961), p. 105.

Worm is the "anti-Mahood" (346) in the shape of a "tiny blur" (358). As a surrogate for the Unnamable, Worm is accorded spatial circumstances similar to those assumed by the Unnamable at the beginning of his narration. Worm is the "tiny blur" located in the "depths of the pit" (358). He is also placed at the center of a circle whose circumference is determined by the position of the "delegates"; no matter where Worm goes, "being at the center, he will go towards them. So he is at the centre, there is a clue of the highest interest, it matters little to what" (356).

However, despite Worm's apparent dimensionlessness and his ideal location, Worm has an eye with which he can see the lights of the "delegates" and he is able to hear their voices. This first faculty is a sign that Worm must exist in space. He too cannot be at the center of the circle. More importantly, his ability to hear the "delegates" indicates that Worm is made of words, no less a fiction than Mahood: "But is it them he hears? Are they really necessary that he may hear, they and kindred puppets" (359). Thus the paradise of selfhood that Worm was supposed to occupy, a "safe place ... not like Eden" (348), turns out to be like the Biblical Eden, for Worm will be expelled from it by the voices. Indeed, Worm, conceived in words, could never have been there. Worm cannot be the self that would end the Unnamable's quest, and so his story is aborted.

No matter what expedient the Unnamable chooses he cannot resolve the contradictory nature of his existence: both outside of space and within space. Playing on the literal meaning of the word, he terms his prison of words a "parlour": "... there is nowhere but here, there are not two places, there are not two prisons, it's my parlour, it's a parlour, where I wait for nothing ..." (410). However, the self enclosed with the Unnamable's parlor is but a fictional self; his real self lies in the silence beyond its limits, "a wordless thing in an empty place" (386): "... there is nothing but here, and the silence outside, nothing but this voice and the silence all around, no need of walls, yes, we must have walls, I need walls good and thick, I need a

prison, I was right, for me alone, I'll go there now, I'll put
me in it, I'm there already, I'll start looking for me now,
I'm there somewhere, it won't be I, no matter, I'll say
it's I . . ." (410). The Unnamable's only hope is to continue
his narration until he hits upon the words that will find
him in the void.

V

The journey to the empty core of being started in *Molloy*
has thus been a failure. The protagonists of the trilogy have
come increasingly closer to seizing the dimensionless self
but have been able to take the final step across the threshold separating space from non-space, existence from the
void. The shape of the trilogy reflects that journey. As
the outside world crumbles away and the narrators of the
trilogy are progressively "refined out of existence,"[18] the trilogy contracts within itself like a spiral decreasing in am-
plitude.

The reclusion of Molloy and Malone demonstrates a rejection of external reality. Confined to a room, exchanging
the space of the macrocosm for that of the microcosm, they
turn inward toward their own speculations on the nature
of consciousness. Recalling another recluse, Marcel Proust,
they seek self-knowledge and, with it, salvation through
their writing. Yet the literature they create from the fragments of the world to which they have died only perpetuates their exile from self.

Continuing the excavations of his predecessors, the Unnamable descends to the edge of the void. And when he can
advance no farther, he bitterly laments that he has reached
the mind's deepest zone — "stupid obsession with depth"
(293) — aware that he cannot forestall seeking an escape
from his present impasse. Indeed, we see the Unnamable

---

[18] Melvin J. Friedman, "Samuel Beckett and the Nouveau Roman,"
Wisconsin Studies in Contemporary Literature, 1 (Spring-Summer
1960), 28.

beginning to recreate the trilogy in his vain attempt to say where he is. His solipsistic voice continues to speak with space-bound words that create the "elsewhere" of fiction. It is the distance, however minimal, between the spaceless "here" of the self and the "elsewhere" that keeps the trilogy from the silence to which it aspires.

CHAPTER II

JOURNEY WITHOUT END

I

MOVEMENT IS ONE OF THE MEANS by which the human personality organizes the world: we move from one point to another with a view toward attaining a certain goal and, in so doing, we determine a path as well as a direction. Since movement generally signifies the traversing of a certain space within a given period of time, and the passage of time is concomitant with an accumulation of experiences, human life has often been represented as a voyage or a quest. Of course, human beings and other living creatures are not the only source of movement in the world. The cosmos itself is in constant motion, and it is from the movements of the heavenly bodies that we derive our notion of time — the objective time of clocks and calendars.

Hugh Kenner has compared Beckett's characters to "Newtonian bodies"; [1] their mobility or immobility at a given moment is almost always a matter of considerable importance. Moreover, one must take into account how certain movements are effected: unaided or with the help of machines, upright or on the ground, smooth and effortless, or convulsive and painfully difficult. Within the trilogy, movement and stasis come to represent two conflicting

---

[1] Hugh Kenner, *Samuel Beckett: A Critical Study* (New York: Grove Press, 1961), p. 25.

modes of being whose opposition is an essential aspect of the quest for self.

II

Although Molloy attributes his compulsion to journey toward his mother's room to the "imperative" (86) of an inner voice, his movement is synonymous with life-in-time. It is woven into the fabric of existence. The wheel of life bears him along: "...my movements owed nothing to the places they caused to vanish, but were due to something else, to the buckled wheel that carried me, in unforeseeable jerks, from fatigue to rest and inversely..." (66). In as much as his mother set the wheel in motion when she brought Molloy into the world, Molloy's journey of life takes the form of a voyage to her room, a voyage that can be terminated only when Molloy has died to the world: "...all my life, I think I had been going to my mother, with the purpose of establishing our relations on a less precarious footing. And when I was with her, and I often succeeded, I left her without having done anything. And when I was no longer with her I was again on my way to her, hoping to do better the next time. And when I appeared to give up and to busy myself with something else, or with nothing at all any more, in reality I was hatching my plans and seeking the way to her house" (87).

But even as a foetus Molloy disliked motion: "And I forgive her [Mag] for having jostled me a little during the first few months..." (18). True stasis is possible, however, only in the void of the self, within which time and movement have finally been halted: "...here nothing stirs, has ever stirred, will ever stir, except myself, who do not stir either when I am there..." (40).

The bicycle (one of the old-fashioned chainless kind) Molloy uses during the first part of his journey serves two purposes: it is both a means of locomotion and a means of support. It supplements Molloy's defective body by transferring the energy he puts into pedaling into a mechanical movement considerably more efficient than the unaided motion of the human body could be — and far more so than Molloy's crippled body. Mounted on his bicycle, his body assimilated to a machine developped through the ingenuity of the human mind, Molloy offers to the observer an idealized image of man, unfettered by infirmity, triumphant on a mechanical steed. Molloy happily recalls the horn he used to herald his approach: "To blow this horn was for me a real pleasure, almost a vice. I will go further and declare that if I were obliged to record, in a roll of honour, those activities which in the course of my interminable existence have given me only a mild pain in the balls, the blowing of a rubber horn — toot! — would figure among the first" (16).

This ideal image is but an illusion, one that becomes transparently obvious when Molloy rests on his bicycle. At such moments Molloy is able to assume a modified foetal position (recalling his desire to be back in his mother's room) which he calls his "raglimp stasis" (26) — "astride my bicycle, my arms on the handlebars, my head on my arms" (20). Here the bicycle prevents Molloy from collapsing, or, as Hugh Kenner puts it, bicycle and man mingle in "conjoint stasis"; the bicycle "extends and stabilizes Molloy's endoskeleton." [2]

Molloy's "raglimp stasis" does not fool the authorities of the first town he encounters on his route. There Molloy is arrested for improperly resting on his bicycle, and thus setting a bad example for the citizenry. Looking at himself through the eyes of those who condemn him, Molloy modifies his initial description of his resting posture. His legs become useless appendages that merely serve, and barely, to keep the bicycle upright. His head no longer reposes peacefully on his arms but now dangles with the trembling typical of the aged. What we see is a doddering wreck of a man, lassitudinous and debilitated, being supported artificially by a bicycle. The authorities view such a man as a

---

[2] Kenner, p. 118.

menace to security. If the townspeople were to break the spell of their everyday activities they might perceive in Molloy a projection of their own destinies and understand the vanity of their existences: "What is certain is this, that I never rested in that way again, my feet obscenely resting on the earth, my arms on the handlebars and on my arms my head, rocking and abandoned. It is indeed a deplorable sight, a deplorable example for the people, who so need to be encouraged, in their bitter toil and to have before their eyes manifestations of strength only, of courage and of joy, without which they might collapse at the end of the day, and roll on the ground" (24).

At Lousse's house the bicycle stage of Molloy's journey comes abruptly to an end, when he discovers that his machine has suddenly become unserviceable. We are never told whether it is rust or some sort of mechanical failure that transforms the bicycle into a useless assemblage of parts, fit now only for the scrape heap. But what happens to Molloy's bicycle is perhaps the fate of all machines. Beckett's universe, Edith Kern writes, "has lost the conviction that machines are perfect and that man may strive for perfection with their help. In this world, machines — whether human bodies or bicycles — decay and remain as sheer memories." [3]

Molloy's departure from Lousse's house signals the second phase of his journey, that of the man on crutches. Having lost one machine, he has turned to another. Like his bicycle, Molloy's crutches can be utilized as a means of support, enabling Molloy to remain erect, that is, to rest without having to lie down — "drooping between my crutches, sleeping on my feet" (22) — and, of course, as a means of locomotion. Although Molloy had recalled his bicycle with obvious pleasure, he devotes more attention to his motion on crutches than he did to his bicycle riding. He finds that moving on crutches bears a certain resem-

[3] Edith Kern, "Black Humour: The Pockets of Lemuel Gulliver and Samuel Beckett," in *Samuel Beckett Now*, ed. Melvin J. Friedman (Chicago: University of Chicago Press, 1970), p. 102.

blance to flying: "There is rapture, or there should be, in the motion crutches give. It is a series of little flights skimming the ground. You take off, you land, through the thronging sound in wind and limb, who have to fasten one foot to the ground before they dare lift up the other. And even their most joyous hastening is less aerial than my hobble. But these are reasonings based on analysis" (64). Molloy himself is conscious of the flaw in his description. The change from the affirmative "there is rapture" to the conditional "there should be" and the avowal "these are reasonings based on analysis" reveal that Molloy can compare his progression on crutches to flying only if he abstracts from it the painful expenditure of energy necessary to propel his body through the air. He may care to *think* of himself as an airplane, taking off and landing with a freedom and grace that scoff at the clumsy earth-bound pedestrian, but, in reality, his crutches are a far less efficient machine than was his bicycle and their use requires a much greater physical exertion. By continuing to eliminate the part his body plays in moving him forward on his crutches, Molloy can maintain that he does not regret the loss of his bicycle: "I didn't feel I missed my bicycle, no, not really, I didn't mind going on the way I said, swinging low in the dark over the earth, along the little empty country roads" (66).

As Molloy's body degenerates during the course of his voyage, there is an accompanying degeneration in his movement. Molloy forgets about "reasonings based on analysis" and admits that his progress "slow and painful at all times" (76) has become even slower and more painful.[4] When Molloy enters the forest there is a marked deterioration in his progression. He covers little ground, his halts become more frequent, and his motion becomes erratic and con-

---

[4] An image relating to the degeneration of Molloy's movement has been lost in the English. In the French, Molloy's earlier "vols" (97) give way to the more erratic "voltiges": "Car je ne savais plus sur quel pied me poser entre mes voltiges" (117). The English keeps the former but translates this last sentence as: "For I didn't know which foot to land on when I came down" (77).

vulsive: "... I hobble, listen, fall, rise, listen and hobble on ..." (78). Beckett leaves it to the reader to imagine how Molloy passes from a vertical position to a horizontal one and back to the vertical.

In time, Molloy is no longer able to properly use his crutches, for they sink into the soft, rain-soaked leaves on the forest floor and must be disengaged with each oscillation. But these difficult conditions are not what makes Molloy abandon his crutches as such: "But leaves or no," Molloy remarks, "I would have abandoned erect motion, than of man" (89). He begins to worm his way across the forest floor, using his crutches as grapnels. The latter constitute the simplest of the machines that Molloy uses; they require an enormous output of energy on his part, but the resultant movement is spasmodic and tediously slow: "Flat on my belly ... I plunged them ahead of me into the undergrowth, and when I felt they had a hold, I pulled myself forward, with an effort of the wrists. For my wrists were still quite strong, fortunately, in spite of my decrepitude, though all swollen and racked by a kind of chronic arthritis probably" (89-90). This new mode of locomotion, however painful and dehumanized it may be, is not without its consolations: "But he who moves this way, crawling on his belly, like a reptile, no sooner comes to rest than he begins to rest, and even the very movement is a kind of rest, compared to other movements, I mean those that have worn me out" (90). With nothing to bolster him, there can be no repose for Molloy, standing, seated, or kneeling. Only stretched out horizontally, with the weight of his body totally supported, can he find some semblance of rest. But Molloy does carry with him a souvenir of better days, in the horn he removed from his bicycle when he left Lousse's house. But it too is deteriorating: "From time to time I blew my horn, through the cloth of my pocket. Its toot was fainter every time" (89).

Collapsed in a ditch at the edge of the forest, Molloy wonders how he can cross the plain that now separates him from his mother's room: "For how could I drag myself over that vast moor, where my crutches would fumble in vain. Rolling perhaps" (91). It might be possible for Molloy, transformed into a great cylinder, to roll for a short distance. But in order to reach his mother's room, he would need an ideal world, one in which his body would be perfectly streamlined and in which there would be no friction and no obstacles to impede the cylinder once it began to roll. Such a world does not exist, of course, and Molloy has to be transported to his mother's room: "I don't know how I got there. Perhaps in an ambulance, certainly in a vehicle of some kind" (7).

Molloy had previously associated being transported with failure and with death. During the night he spent sitting behind the boulder, he had wondered about the fate of C, the vagabond with whom he sympathizes and whom he resembles. When dawn came, he questioned whether C was in one of the carts coming to market, "overcome by fatigue or discouragement, perhaps even dead" (15). Molloy too is "dead," in the sense that his immobility in the ditch marks the end of the journey of life. As for the obscure powers that provide his transportation, their intervention reminds us that we are in a world of fiction and that Molloy must reach his mother's room in order to begin his story.

It is evident that the metamorphosis Molloy undergoes during the course of his journey, from the man on the bicycle to the bedridden invalid in his mother's room, follows a specific progression. One aspect of this progression has been termed by Hugh Kenner the "dismembering of the Cartesian centaur." [5] As Kenner points out, Descartes, writing within the framework of a mechanistic view of the universe — and, we may add, during a period which saw a great development in the mechanical sciences — conceived of man's body as "a machine created by the hand of God, and in consequence incomparably better designed and with more admirable movements than any machine invented by man." [6] Despite this definition, Descartes admits that the

---

[5] Kenner, p. 131.
[6] René Descartes, *Discourse on Method*, in *Discourse on Method and Meditations*, trans. Laurence Lafleur (New York: The Library of Liberal Arts, 1964), p. 41.

body suffers pain and is obviously not composed of gears and levers. Moreover, there was the problem of man's dualism, as Descartes postulated it in his philosophy. On the one hand, there is the mind which is pure spirit, and, on the other, there is the body which is part of the material world and like it possesses the qualities of extension, quantity, and movement. Theoretically, then, mind and body should be entirely distinct since spirit cannot be matter nor matter spirit. But Descartes had difficulty explaining how the mind commands the body to perform certain functions, although he posited a point of interpenetration in the pineal gland. Yet if the mind acts on the material body, then it must somehow be material; and if the body reports sense impressions to the mind, then it must at some point be spiritual. Hence the body is something more than a machine, more than an ideal arrangement of matter.

In *Molloy*, Descartes' ideal vision of man is, of course, suggested by Molloy on his bicycle. Here would be a perfect mechanical body commanded by the mind (whose essence, according to Descartes, is reason) without there being any interaction of mind and body. Such a man would be the quintessence of intelligence and order, exempt from pain, sickness, and decay, a godlike figure moving effortlessly over the earth, master of all he surveys.

But, as we have seen, Molloy's "Cartesian centaur" is only an illusion, a tragi-comic caricature of Descartes' ideal man. His "raglimp stasis," the increasing crudeness and inefficiency of the machines he must use, the fading bicycle horn, the concomitant degeneration of his body; all these phenomena testify to the conclusion that there is no obviating the suffering and the deterioration that are an inescapable part of the human condition. Moreover, Molloy is caught up as well in the Cartesian muddle concerning the interpenetration of mind and body: "I stopped to think. It is difficult to think riding, for me. When I try to think riding I lose my balance and fall" (26).

The breakdown in Molloy's motion suggests that he falls victim to yet another process, that of entropy: the "tendency of a well-ordered universe to go over into a state of

disorder" and the "behavior of things [that tend] to become increasingly random."[7] As entropy increases within
a given system, an ever greater amount of energy is re-
quired to maintain some kind of order until, with a final
loss of energy, the system passes into a state of total disorder and inertia.

Mounted on his bicycle, machine and man assimilated
into one unit, Molloy takes up his quest for his mother as
what we might call a well-ordered universe in miniature.
His motion is organized, efficient, and well directed. When
Molloy switches from his bicycle to his crutches as his principal means of locomotion, the precise movements of pedal
and wheel give way to the abrupt thrust and jerk of poles
against the ground. Although Molloy puts more energy into
moving, his movements are considerably more haphazard.
With the use of his crutches as grapnels, Molloy's system
approaches the brink of disorder. Molloy has lost most of
the mechanical advantage that his other machines had pro-
vided and must now pull the entire weight of his body forward along the ground. As for the direction of Molloy's
motion, it has become even more random. And at times
Molloy closes his eyes and, literally, plunges blindly ahead.
By the time he emerges from the forest he has lost the
fight against entropy and collapses inert in a ditch.

Thus life-in-time is an entropic journey. Molloy's body-
machine, whether we care to consider it within the context
of Cartesianism or simply to use the image of the machine
as a simile for the body's aggregate of systems, is doomed
to run down and rejoin the inert matter from which it
sprang, passing from order to disorder and then to stasis.
Entropy, many physicists believe, will be the fate of the
entire universe. Relatively speaking, the universe is eternal,
whereas man is finite: his entropy does not require bil-

---

[7] Wylie Sypher, *Loss of the Self in Modern Literature and Art*
(New York: Vintage Books, 1964), p. 73. For the theme of entropy
in modern fiction see also Alvin Greenberg, "The Novel of Disintegration: Paradoxical Impossibility in Modern Fiction," *Wisconsin
Studies in Contemporary Literature*, 7 (Winter-Spring 1966), 103-124.

lions of years but only three score and ten. It is therefore
not surprising that Molloy gives up the upright position
proper to man for crawling on his stomach like a worm.
Having lost the means by which he shored up his sagging
body, there is no reason why he should support the burden
of being a man when the journey of life has been a de-
humanizing process, a calvary that no man should endure.

. We can place the disintegration of Molloy's movement
in still another context: that of man as *homo faber*. If
there has ever been an age that has placed its faith in machines, it is the twentieth century with its labor-saving
devices, rapid means of transport, and sophisticated "hard-
ware." As Paule-Y. Reye has demonstrated in her article
"Machine and Art," the depiction of machines and man-
machines in the works of such modern artists as Fernand
Léger and Hans Erni reveals an underlying confidence in
technological man, who by virtue of his inventions will be
able to dominate the universe. Commenting on Erni's paint-
ing *The Fall of Icarus*, Reye remarks that for Erni modern
man with his machines will not suffer the fate of Daedalus'
son: "Icarus will no longer fall from his proud heights
when he knows how to work the compass and the slide
rule." [8] Beckett does not share Erni's optimism. The modern
Icarus will fall just as Molloy falls, for however sophisticated man's machines may be, they cannot change his lot in a
cruel and inhuman universe.

One of the means that Molloy employs — in addition to
his machines — to resist the disintegration and disorder of
his voyage is the application of geometry. At certain moments of his journey he attempts to impose his will and
intelligence upon his movements by giving them the shape
of a regular geometric figure. For Descartes, of course, the
study of mathematics constituted the noblest demonstra-
tion of man's reason. Later developments in the sciences
extended Descartes' faith in man's ability to extend himself
into the cosmos and encompass it within logical constructs

---

[8] Paul-Y. Reye, "Machine et art," *Revue d'esthétique* 16 (January-
March 1963), 292.

that would obey the fundamental laws of mathematics. But Molloy is imprisoned in a world of chance and imperfection where will, logic, and resolution are but the vestiges of an antiquated egocentrism.

Faced with the problem of finding his way out of the city in which he met Lousse, Molloy attempts to travel in a straight line: "And it seemed to me that if I kept on in a straight line I was bound to leave it, sooner or later. So I set myself to this as best I could, making allowance for the drift to the right of the feeble light that was my guide. And my pertinancy was such that I did indeed come to the ramparts as night was falling, having described a good quarter of a circle through bad navigation" (65). But later, when Molloy wishes to leave the forest, he remembers having read somewhere "that when a man in a forest thinks he is going forward in a straight line, in reality he is going in a circle" (85). Therefore Molloy takes the converse of what he had read and decides to travel in a circle, hoping in this way to end up moving in a straight line. [9] His path turns out to be neither a straight line nor a circle: "But there was always present to my mind, which was still working, if laboriously, the need to turn, to keep on turning, and every three or four jerks I altered course, which permitted me to describe, if not a circle, at least a great polygon, perfection is not of this world . . ." (90). The ship metaphors that Molloy uses in both these instances are significant. Molloy might like to steer a perfect course to his mother's room, using mathematics to determine his direction, but his ship is adrift.

---

[9] Cf. Descartes, *Discourse on Method*: "My second maxim was to be as firm and determined in my actions as I could be, and not to act on the most doubtful decisions, once I had made them, any less resolutely than on the most certain. In this matter I patterned my behavior on that of travelers, who, finding themselves lost in a forest, must not wander about . . . but should go as straight as they can in the direction they first select and not change the direction except for the strongest reasons. By this method, even if the direction was chosen at random, they will presumably arrive at some destination, not perhaps where they would like to be, but at least where they will be better off than in the middle of the forest." trans. Lafleur, p. 19.

Looked at as a whole, Molloy's entire journey is no less imperfect than his attempts at navigation. Within the restricted space of his region, his movements describe a strange path. Leaving the hill from which he observed A and C, he voyages toward the city where his mother's room is to be found but apparently misses it. He then goes as far as the coast, at which point he must turn back toward the interior and once more head for his mother's city. Moreover, we know that this is not Molloy's first journey: he has visited his mother on previous occasions, passed through the forest at least once before, and recalls a previous sojourn at the seashore. At one point in his narration Molloy terms these haphazard and repetitive mouvements "spirals" (68), as if to confer upon them some regularity. But their real shape, as he notes earlier, is that of "devious winding ways" (60). [10] Molloy's movements cannot be made to coincide with a regular configuration; they are a hit-and-miss affair, an *ad hoc* progression that defies logic and categorization.

At only one point during his voyage does Molloy establish a relationship between his movement and time. This occurs during his stay at Lousse's house when he uncovers a puzzling disparity between his movement and the rythms of the world around him. This disparity is the first element of a complex spatio-kinetic image by which Beckett portrays "the continuity-in-change of self and its relationship with external reality." [11] Life-in-time, inseparable from movement, signifies the evanescence of the personality, and the only continuity possible is to be found in the void, from which movement is absent.

On the first night of his stay at Lousse's house, Molloy awakens during the night and from his barred window observes the passage of the moon across the sky. For a

---

[10] The French "boucles complexes et informes" (91) is less poetic than "devious winding ways" but provides a sharper contrast with the spiral configuration Molloy would like his movements to describe.

[11] Ross Chambers, "Samuel Beckett and the Padded Cell," *Meanjin Quarterly*, 21 (December 1962), 455.

brief moment, the moon is framed in the window, whose
two bars divide the moon into three sections. Molloy no-
tices that the section on the right grows larger as the section on the left grows smaller, with the middle section
remaining the same. Molloy deduces the obvious — that the
moon is moving. Upon further analysis, however, the situation appears uncertain: the room may be stationary and
the moon moving, or vice versa, or both the room and the
moon may be moving, but at different speeds and in different directions. Since there is no way for Molloy to stand
outside the system constituted by the moon and the room
in order to arrive at some objective conclusion, Molloy is
left to confront a relativistic situation of "an extreme com-
plexity" (39).

Molloy has been traveling ever since he left the lee of
his boulder, and the moon has been on the move as well.
Both movements yield a certain quantity of time elapsed:
in the case of Molloy, three days; and in the case of the
moon, fourteen days, for Molloy recalls that the moon was
new when he departed and the moon he sees from his
window is a full moon. Somehow, Molloy's time scale is
different from the objective time of the universe. We may
infer that the universe has not changed but that Molloy
has: Molloy's time has slowed down, thus making everything appear to move more quickly.

Faced with this disparity in chronology, Molloy is dis-
mayed and mystified. Other phenomena reinforce his temporal disorientation. On the same night that Molloy observed the moon passing outside his window, he also noticed
the movement of the trees outside his room: "They rocked
gently, but not all the time, shaken now and then by sudden spasms" (42). On the following morning, a change in
the movement of the trees reveals another variance between
Molloy's time and that of external reality. They are now
wildly agitated: "The boughs themselves seemed to shift,
as though endowed with an orbital velocity of their own..."
(44).

Molloy is also puzzled by certain movements taking
place within Lousse's house. The doorway of his room is

at first framed in the opaque window of the landing just outside it. Later, something moves to change the position of the room with respect to the rest of the house: "... in the big frosted window the door was no longer inscribed, but had slightly shifted to the right, or to the left, I forget ..." (44). Molloy dismisses the change as a quirk of nature, telling himself that the "ressources of nature are infinite" (44).

When Molloy sums up his stay at Lousse's house he states that in all probability he occupied a series of rooms, and then explains: "The house was fixed, that is perhaps what I mean by these different rooms" (51). The juxtaposition of "different rooms" and "fixed" suggests that the occupation of several rooms signifies a movement of some kind as opposed to the immobility of the house. If we take Molloy's passage from one room to another as a representation of the period of time he spent at Lousse's house, then the second term of the equation would be the motionlessness of the house, signifying permanence and timelessness. Since the rooms are within the house, we have diversity within uniformity, change within permanence. We can add to these elements the "parading universe" (51) Molloy observes from his room, and which, as we have already seen, has its own rate of movement.

As for Molloy himself, when he is "still" he is "fixed" like the house, frozen in time and space. And when he moves, he moves so slowly as to have the impression of being "in a cage out of time ... and out of space to be sure" (51). This extremely slow movement refers back to Molloy's changing rooms, and hence the house would be the timeless and spaceless cage to which Molloy alludes.

The room serves here as a metaphor for the self, and thus the series of rooms Molloy inhabits represent the self changing in time as Molloy passes from one room to another. Such a change begins to take place even before Molloy switches rooms, as revealed by the change in the position of the doorway of Molloy's first room. However, we know that Molloy's essential self is atemporal and aspatial, subject to neither change nor movement. Lousse's house is thus analogous to Molloy's real self. The slowness of Molloy's movement approaches the immobility of the house, reinforcing the notion that Molloy's time has slowed down. With time running down, the self that operates in the everyday world comes to resemble the real self. Hence at Lousse's house Molloy experiences an approximation of the void that true and lasting stasis would bring into being.

Molloy confronts another dilemma concerning time when his voyage is over. Lying immobile in his mother's room, dead to external reality, he has come closer to stopped time. He now finds himself in a twilight zone somewhere between death and the end of time: "My life, my life, now I speak of it as something over, now as of a joke that still goes on, and is there any tense for that? (36). The timelessness Molloy wishes to attain is eternity, but an eternity that is more than simple duration without end. As Saint Bonaventure defined it: "If one says that eternity signifies existence without end, we must reply that this does not exhaust the word eternity; for the latter does not only mean endlessness but also simultaneity." [12] Molloy was referring to this same simultaneity of past and present, when he described the void of consciousness as a "world at an end," whose termination was occasioned by its beginning and vice versa. Similarly, if birth coincides with death and death with birth, then the time interval between them is abolished and one "lives" outside of time.

If Molloy had the tense he seeks, one that is "somewhere between past and present, that will express a past more recent than yesterday but not quite simultaneous with today," [13] he might hope to capture the merging of past and present and thus describe his passage from temporality to atemporality. Such a tense is lacking, and in a larger sense it is the very nature of language that is at fault. Bound to a temporal world, language is as incapable of expressing

---

[12] Quoted by Georges Poulet, *Les Métamorphoses du cercle* (Paris: Plon, 1961), p. v.

[13] Chambers, "Beckett's Brinkmanship," in *Samuel Beckett: A Collection of Critical Essays*, ed. Martin Esslin (Englewood Cliffs, New Jersey: Spectrum Books, 1965), p. 161.

timelessness as it was incapable of capturing spacelessness. Moreover, the very act of writing perpetuates Molloy's temporality. His "mythological present" (26) results, as its appelation reveals, from his inability to make his past (what he describes) coincide with his present (the moment of writing); for no sooner are his words written then the moment they attempt to seize has already become part of the past.

Another dilemma concerning time that Molloy must also face is that the closer he comes to stopped time, the slower time passes and hence the farther his goal withdraws from him. Thus his existence becomes "interminable" (16) and the story of his life stretches into an "enormous history" (18). His physical journey gives way to a period of endless waiting for the end of time. However, recalling Molloy's inability to ride his bicycle and think at the same time, when Molloy stops moving he begins to write. Seen from this perspective, his waiting is transformed into another sort of voyage: Molloy must now wonder interminably through the vast reaches of language, ceaselessly relating fictions in his attempt to find his self and thus fall silent.

Moran's voyage extends Molloy's. Its analogies with the latter both reveal Moran's growing resemblance to Molloy and suggest that his mission is a trial-run for a future voyage that will duplicate Molloy's. In Moran's story, Molloy's "imperative" is replaced by Youdi's order to find Molloy. The announcement of the mission shatters the stillness of a Sunday morning, forcing Moran to foresake the peace of his garden and plunging him into the agitation of preparing to depart: "All was still. Not a breath. From my neighbour's chimneys the smoke rose straight and blue. None but tranquil sounds, the clicking of mallet and ball, a rake on pebbles, a distant lawn-mower, the bell of my beloved church. And birds of course ... their song sadly dying, vanquished by the heat, and leaving dawn's high boughs for the bushes' gloom. Contentedly I inhaled the scent of my lemon-verbena. In such surroundings slipped away my last moments of peace and happiness" (93).

The significance of Gaber's message is revealed by the nervous movements of Moran's body: "And yet the poison was already acting on me, the poison I had just been given. I stirred restlessly in my arm-chair, ran my hands over my face, crossed and uncrossed my legs, and so on" (96). For Youdi's order is the projection of an inner necessity that Moran can no longer restrain. The Molloy element within him has begun to transmit its movement. Indeed, Moran's conception of Molloy is in terms of motion: "He was forever on the move. I had never seen him at rest" (113). And when Molloy makes his presence felt, he literally moves Moran: "He panted. He had only to rise up within me for me to be filled with panting" (113).

Like Molloy, Moran is trapped in a paradox. He must be on the move but, above all, he desires stasis. As we have already noted, Moran rejects the "turmoil" and "frenzy" of external reality but nonetheless must function amid its turbulence. Opposed to the latter is the stillness of his room and, more importantly, the "slow and massive" world of his mind, where things move with the "ponderous sullenness of oxen" (111). At a deeper level of his consciousness, the zone where the real Molloy is to be found, this slow motion, Beckett suggests, will give way to the motionlessness of the self as Molloy described it. But first Moran must complete the journey to the end of time.

The presence of Molloy within Moran has also given Moran a stiff and painful knee — a reduced form of Molloy's infirmity — which obliges him to use machines to aid his locomotion. Thus Moran has his son purchase a bicycle. That Moran's bicycle is the modern variety — compared to Molloy's older and less efficient chainless kind — emphasizes the degeneration and aging that await Moran if he is to become the one whom he is pursuing. Although designated as the property of his son, the bicycle has been bought for the benefit of Moran; and like Molloy, Moran considers his mechanical steed with a good deal of fondness: "I would gladly write a thousand words on it alone" (155). Moran does not permit himself this pleasure, but he does give careful attention to the bicycle's bell, the instrument that will announce the approach of the man-machine: "... I might have told him [Moran *fils*] to be careful about the bell, to unscrew the little cap and examine it well inside, so as to make sure it was a good bell and in good working order, before concluding the transaction, and to ring it to hear the ring it made" (145). [14]

Man and machine combine differently in the case of Moran, who has his son pedal for him while he sits on the baggage-rack. Yet Moran senses that his elation at being able to ride off with his son on the bicycle is ephemeral. Never again would everything conspire to facilitate his journey: "Happily it was downhill. Happily I had mended my hat, or the wind would have blown it away. Happily the weather was fine and I was no longer alone. Happily, happily" (157). Obviously, Moran is still far from Molloy, who must assume the burden of his own infirmity as he pursues his Cartesian dream. But Moran foresees a future moment when he will no longer be dependent upon his son and have to share a bicycle with him: "I had told him to keep an eye out ... for a second bicycle, light and inexpensive. For I was weary of the carrier and I also saw the day approaching when my son would no longer have the strength to pedal for the two of us. And I believed I was capable, with a little practice, of learning to pedal with one leg. And then I would resume my rightful place, I mean in the van. And my son would follow me" (161).

The departure of Moran's son eliminates the possibility of having company on future voyages and also forces Moran to do without a bicycle on his present voyage. Consequently, Moran's movement begins to break down, for he must now rely upon his umbrella, used as a cane, to help him make

---

[14] Molloy's age and debilitude no doubt cause him to show greater reverence for his bicycle than Moran. The difference between the two protagonists is revealed by Molloy's refusal to call his bicycle a "bike" (16). However, the distinction in French between *bicyclette* and the familiar *vélo* is only partially maintained in the English translation. In the original Molloy states: "Chère bicyclette, je ne t'appellerai pas vélo..." (21). By contrast, Moran speaks of a "vélo tout flambant neuf" (222). This last phrase appears in the English as "a nice brand-new bicycle" (144).

the painful journey home. Although little more than a simple lever, it supplements Moran's body both at rest and in motion: "And I practiced walking with the help of my umbrella. And though in this way I moved no faster and no less painfully, at least I did not tire so quickly. And instead of having to stop every ten steps to rest, I easily managed fifteen, before having to stop. And even while I rested my umbrella was a help. For I found that when I leaned upon it the heaviness in my leg . . . disappeared even more quickly than when I stood supported only by my muscles and the tree of life" (147-148). Like Molloy, Moran must pay the price for the loss of his bicycle. His movement is now less organized and he must expend a greater amount of energy in order to cover the same distance he once traversed so easily on his bicycle. Moran is experiencing in attenuated form the disintegration and entropy to which Molloy fell victim and which will no doubt become Moran's lot. Similarly, as we saw in the preceding chapter, Moran's method of gathering up his keys approximates modes of locomotion that Molloy had employed. We may infer from the nature of Moran's voyage that one day he will have recourse to these types of movement. The final analogy between the two voyages is revealed by Moran's learning to use crutches after he has returned home in order to prepare himself for a new departure: "I am clearing out. . . . I have crutches now. I shall go faster, all will go faster" (175).

There are other voyagers whom Moran comes to resemble. Moran's hobbling on his cane associates him with two other vagabonds — C and the first passerby who enters Moran's camp site. The former walks with an uncertain step, and with his cane "crushing the silent grass, pounding the silent ground" (15), strikes out against the mute cruelty of the universe. The second tramp anticipates Moran's reliance on his cane by permitting Moran to hold his staff. C and the passerby are twin aspects of one character and present an intermediate stage of the journey upon which Moran is irrevocably embarked.

Moran appears destined to discover that once his travels properly speaking are over, he will continue to wander in search of the words that will enable him to find Molloy. Although Moran is not yet confronted by the problem of describing a life that is over and continuing at the same time, he does discover the time lapse between the moment of writing and the present. Reaching the end of his narration, he writes: "It is midnight. The rain is beating on the windows" (176). A moment later he notes: "It was not midnight. It was not raining" (176). As soon as Moran transcribes the present, it has already become part of the past; and his own time has expanded into the infinite future.

III

Malone, immobile in his bed, begins his narration from where Molloy terminated his. Having once been a voyager, his past presents a fusion of the experiences of his earlier incarnations, Molloy and Moran as well as C and the first passerby. He too has had to undertake an entropic journey, and the vestiges of the machines he used to aid his movement bear witness to the disintegration of the Cartesian centaur and the impotence of *homo faber*. Malone recalls having "wandered in the towns, the woods and wildernesses and tarried by the seas" (225-226). He must have utilized a staff and crutches, for he remembers a period when he was able to travel without their aid; and among his possessions are the "cap of a bicycle bell" and a "half-crutch" (252).

But illusions have a way of persisting: for Malone the dream of moving with the precision and durability of a machine is not completely dead. Faced with the tedium of writing and waiting, Malone envisions transforming his bed into a crude sort of bicycle on which he can depart from his room: "I wonder if I could not contrive, wielding my stick like a punt-pole, to move my bed. It may well be on castors, many beds are. Incredible I should never have thought of this, all the time I have been here. I might even succeed in steering it, it is so narrow, through the door, and even down the stairs, if there is a stairs that goes down. To be off and away" (253). Malone's speculations upon voyaging forth on his bed are no less fanciful than Archimedes' boast that he could move the earth if he were given a point in space and a suitable lever. Malone-Archimedes loses his stick, and with it the possibility of making anything but a verbal journey: "The bed has not stirred. I must have missed my point of purchase, in the dark. Sine qua non, Archimedes was right. The stick, having slipped, would have plucked me from the bed if I had not let it go" (254). But if Malone himself is unable to move, there remains the motion of his "homuncules."

Sapo, like Molloy, is obliged to move by an inner imperative, pushed along by forces beyond his control: ". . . they watched him depart, on stumbling, wavering feet, as though they scarcely felt the ground. Often he stopped, stood tottering a moment, then suddenly was off again in a new direction. So he went, limp, drifting, as though tossed by the earth. And when, after a halt, he started off again, it was like a big thistledown plucked by the wind from the place where it had settled" (196). And Sapo stops "simply because the voice had ceased that told him to go on" (206). As Sapo ages the journey of life will grow more spasmodic as debilitude and entropy increase with the passage of time: "But these stations were short-lived, for he was still young. And of [sic] a sudden he is off again, on his wanderings, passing from light to shadow, from shadow to light, unheedingly" (206).

Such a progression is evinced by Macmann as he continues the journey of his younger precedessor. Forced to "go on coming and going on the earth . . . for obscure reasons known who knows to God alone" (245), Macmann wishes only to remain motionless: ". . . happier sitting than standing and lying down than sitting, so that he sat and lay down at the least pretext . . ." (243).

Fitfully pushed on by the wheel of life, Macmann finds that his path is a *via dolorosa* paved with shards and excrement, as if his fellow men and the universe were conspiring to place still other obstacles in his path: "For he was incapable of picking his steps and choosing where to put down his feet (which would have permitted him to go barefoot). And even had he been so he would have been so to no great purpose, so little was he master of his movements. And what is the good of aiming at the smooth and mossy places when the foot, missing its mark, comes down on the flints and shards or sinks up to the knee in the cowpads" (245).

When Macmann is too weak to employ the upright position, he inches along the ground, like Molloy with his grapnels or Moran when he gathers together his keys, reduced to a creature less than human: "And sometimes you cannot, get to your feet I mean, and have to drag yourself to the nearest plot of vegetables, using the tufts of grass and asperities of the earth to drag yourself forward..." (232-233).

Macmann's solitary and painful journey is the voyage of Everyman, and the way in which men move testifies to the loneliness and cruelty of existence. Beckett contrasts the movements of men with the movements of the waves: "...the spasms of waves from shore to shore all stirring to their tiniest stir, and the so different motion of men... who are not tied together, but free to come and go as they please" (233). Men may be isolated one from another, if that is their freedom, but in other respects their movements are severely limited by laws and processes over which an individual has no control. For example, the body, the instrument of movement, is a far cry from the perfect machine Descartes imagined. Not only is its movement deficient, but disease and infirmity inevitably cause it to cease functioning. "Their great balls and sockets rattling like knackers," men move along, "each on his way." "And when one dies the others go on, as if nothing had happened" (233).

As one of those defective machines, Macmann dreams of escaping his condition. Just as Molloy once imagined he might be able to roll to his mother's house, Macmann wonders if he can advance by rolling along the ground. His speculations extend those of Molloy, for Macmann sees himself transformed into some quintessential Cartesian machine, his streamlined body turning effortlessly with no interpenetration of mind and body: "And without reducing his speed he began to dream of a flat land where he would never have to rise again and hold himself erect in equilibrium, first on the right foot for example, then on the left, and where he might come and go and so survive after the fashion of a great cylinder endowed with the faculties of cognition and volition" (246). Like all similar notions that Beckett's protagonists permit themselves to entertain, Macmann's dream can only be realized in a make-believe world. The recurrence of the desire to move with the ease and grace of a synchronized god serves to emphasize the harsh and incomprehensible nature of existence in the macrocosm.

As we saw predicted in the case of Sapo, Macmann's halts become more frequent and of longer duration. Yet as old as Macmann is, he too has his "enormous history" in which even a long "station" becomes but a brief moment: "But it must not be thought he will never move again out of this place and attitude, for he still has the whole of his old age before him, and then that kind of epilogue, when it is not very clear what is happening..." (232). The "epilogue" in question refers, of course, to the period of endless waiting that follows the protagonist's final immobility. But it is Malone, Macmann's creator, who must wait in his room and attempt to terminate the journey.

IV

"No, once and for all," the Unnamable announces, "I do not move" (292). Pure consciousness is a state in which time and movement, attributes of external reality, do not exist. The Unnamable has never been anywhere; he is immobile, "riveted" (409) in the void. If he does speak of time, it is because language is bound to a temporal world. Thus time is a notion inflicted upon the Unnamable by his "delegates": "I say years, though here there are no years. . . . Years is one of Basil's ideas" (309).

And given the contradictory existence of the Unnamable there exists movement where there should be none — that of his fictional castoffs and of his "vice-existers." The two types of movement presented by the Unnamable's discarded fictions yield two different concepts of time. First and most important is Malone who, though himself immobile, "appears and disappears with the punctuality of clockwork, always at the same remove, the same velocity, in the same direction, the same attitude" (294). His motionlessness and the regularity of his orbit reveal the Unnamable's inability to represent timelessness. As Richard Coe notes: " 'Timelessness' is in fact time which moves in circles. 'Eternity' can only be conceived as finite sequences of time infinitely repeated." [15] Opposed to Malone are the other fictional castoffs that surround the Unnamable: "Others come towards me, pass before me, wheel about me" (299). Their irregular movements would seem to indicate that they have been left adrift in time without their temporality ever having been resolved (or supposedly so) as was the case with Malone.

When the Unnamable turns once more to fiction in his search for the self, the "vice-existers" that come into being are perforce temporal incarnations and thus endowed with movement — which attests to the continuing exile of their creator. The "loosing" of a "pseudo-self" signifies that yet another fragment of the Unnamable must journey forth: "Perhaps I shall be obliged, in order not to peter out, to invent another fairy-tale, yet another, with heads, trunks, arms, legs and all that follows, let loose in the changeless round of imperfect shadow and dubious light" (307).

Mahood has just enough left of one arm to manipulate a crutch, and with its help he journeys back and forth across his island. He too must obey an "imperative": "The only problem for me was to continue, since I could not do

---

[15] Richard N. Coe, *Samuel Beckett* (New York: Grove Press, 1964), p. 70.

otherwise, to the best of my declining powers, in the motion which had been imparted to me" (320). Mahood's movements are more frenzied and more mechanical than those of his predecessors. Such is the power of the compulsion driving him that when he arrives at the blockhouse where his family resides and finds them dead of food poisoning, he stamps on their bodies and, without interrupting his motion, whirls out the door.

In typical fashion Mahood's journey progressively decays. With the passing years his movement slows down: "He'll never reach us if he doesn't get a move on," his family would remark. "He looks as if he had slowed down since last year" (318). Mahood is the last of the trilogy's travelers, and as such his voyage is a condensation of the other voyages of the trilogy. Thus its final stages are presented in the form of a summary, leaving the reader to speculate upon whether Mahood employed machines other than his crutch and the manner in which he used them to aid his motion, and how he lost his remaining limbs: "For of the great traveller I had been, on my hands and knees in the later stages, then crawling on my belly or sitting on the ground, only the trunk remains (in sorry trim) surmounted by a head . . ." (327).

Although Mahood's journey has no specific destination, he wishes, like Molloy, to impose some coherence upon it. Thus at the beginning of his story, he chooses to describe it as taking the regular form of a spiral. But he later modifies this description and resigns himself, as did Molloy, to the disorder and unintelligibility of his existence: "And my course is not helicoidal, I got that wrong too, but a succession of irregular loops, now sharp and short as in the waltz, now of a parabolic sweep that embraces entire boglands, now between the two, somewhere or other, and invariably unpredictable in direction, that is to say determined by the panic of the moment" (327).

As for Worm, his verbal birth has condemned him to movement. An initial slip of the tongue, as it were, sealed his fate. Only the aborting of his story saves him from his destiny: ". . . a little stir . . . would start things off, the whole fabric would be infected, the ball would start a-rolling, the disturbance would spread to every part, locomotion itself would soon appear, trips properly so called, business trips, pleasure trips, research expeditions, sabbatical leaves, jaunts and rambles, honeymoons at home and abroad and long sad solitary tramps in the rain, I indicate the main trends, athletics, tossing in bed, physical jerks, locomotor ataxy, death throes, rigor and rigor mortis ..." (384).

V

How different is the movement of men from the movement of the sea, Malone remarked, not without a certain envy. The waves roll toward the shore, each one linked indissolubly with those that precede it and those that follow it. And the sea knows no faltering, no infirmity, and no decay. Beckett's wanderers are not blessed with the same companionship and continuity as they travel along the road of life toward the distant paradise of selfhood.

As their voyages progress, their illusions about finding some relief from their calvary are stripped from them and left to become meaningless fossils — like the mute klaxon Molloy keeps with him or the half a bicycle bell Malone unearths from among his paltry possessions. The dream of moving with the grace, precision, and durability of a machine, the naive faith in technology, the belief that man can, through the exercise of his will and intelligence, give coherence and meaning to his existence crumble into absurdity in an absurd universe.

As we penetrate deeper and deeper into the trilogy, the emphasis shifts from the physical voyage to the verbal one. Movement becomes increasingly unreal, increasingly a fiction that the protagonist rejects as belonging to a "pseudoself." Finally, the Unnamable takes us beyond stasis and into an epistemological and linguistic cul-de-sac. Though doomed to futility by its very nature, the quest for self is, nonetheless, a compulsion that cannot be denied. The journey must continue. "I can't go on," the Unnamable murmurs, "I'll go on" (414).

CHAPTER III

THE SOFT LIFE

I

"E FANGO È IL MONDO," Beckett wrote as an epigraph to his prophetic 1931 study of Proust's *A la recherche du temps perdu*, taking this image of the world as mud from Giacomo Leopardi's "A se stesso" — a bitter meditation on the pain of existence in an inhospitable universe. Mud was to become an important element in the landscapes of Beckett's fiction long before its most literal use in *How It Is*.

But as we see in the trilogy the characteristics of mud, softness, amorphousness, and absorbency, are not confined to mud alone. Their occurrence in what appear to be unrelated contexts yields a certain pattern which permits us to better understand the ramifications of *Proust's* epigraph. Opposed to the characteristics of mud are the countervailing properties of hardness, smoothness, and definition, which connote other options, other modes of existence.

The heroes of the trilogy find themselves caught between these alternatives. The "qualities" of their respective existences will reveal just how far they have progressed along the road to selfhood.

II

Molloy takes up his journey on a road whose surface is firm and whose form is well defined, a road that appears

as a "hard and white" (9) scar across the face of the countryside. However, Molloy soon discovers that the landscape
he must cross is not that of a smiling nature. The road
upon which his bicycle once glided gives way to a spongy
surface, while Molloy himself travels with increasing difficulty. More than just the embodiment of a cruel and
incomprehensible universe, the soft tentacles extended by
the landscape transform it into a "soul's landscape"; for
they reflect Molloy's own desire to lay down the burden
of his quest and become one with the earth.

Settling into a ditch to spend the night, Molloy mingles
with the grass as if he wished to become part of the vegetation: "In the ditch the grass was thick and high, I took
off my hat and pressed about my face the long leafy stalks.
Then I could smell the earth, the smell of the earth was
in the grass that my hands wove round my face till I
was blinded. I ate a little too, a little grass" (27). The soft
soil of the ditch lures Molloy with its promise of oblivion:
"But now I shall have to get myself out of this ditch.
How joyfully I would vanish there, sinking deeper and
deeper under the rains" (27). A swamp lying between the
seacoast and his mother's room — which may only be a
"kind of strangled creek which the slow grey tides emptied and filled" (134) — becomes for Molloy both an obstacle and, like the ditch, a temptation. Its proportions are
consequently magnified and it is transformed into a "stinking steaming swamp in which an incalculable number of
human lives were yearly engulfed" (76).[1] By the time Molloy
reaches the forest the landscape has become one of mud.
Having come this far and more conscious than ever of the
"imperative" driving him on, Molloy can no longer hesitate
between moving forward and remaining where he is. The
suction of the mud-like "black and spongy" (89) leaves is
simply an obstacle he must overcome if he is to complete
his journey.

---

[1] The swamp may have a basis in reality — the marshy area
around Dublin.

The reader is told relatively little about the sort of landscape Moran crosses. We do learn, however, that although Moran takes the same roads home "they look different when you go back along them" (165). They are indeed "different" when, during the winter of Moran's return, they are covered with snow. But, more importantly, Moran himself has changed. He is aware that his former mode of existence has been irrevocably lost and he has become the victim of forces he can no longer deny. Thus the snow through which he must force a path is a physical hindrance and also a temptation. Moran might be enticed to sink into the soft snow and abandon his journey: "When a thing resists me, even if it is for my own good, it does not resist me very long. This snow, for example. Though to tell the truth it lured me more than it resisted me" (105).

The landscape is not the only element of Molloy's voyage that lures him with the promise of absorption. The temptations he confronts during his stay with Lousse threaten his pursuit of self and thus stand in direct contrast to the experience of timelessness he undergoes in Lousse's house. With her magic, her dog, and her spurious Garden of Eden, Lousse, though old and ugly, can be identified with Circe and her descendants — the sorceresses of Renaissance romances and their enchanted gardens. [2]

The "softening" of Molloy begins when he awakens to find himself stripped of his armor-like greatcoat, which encloses and protects him like a tough second skin, and clad in a flimsy feminine garment that suggests the passivity Lousse will try to instill in him: "... look at me floating about inside another man's nightdress, another woman's probably, for it was pink and transparent and adorned with ribands and frills and lace" (44). [3]

---

[2] For a comparison between the Lousse episode and the enchanted garden episodes of *Orlando Furioso*, *Jerusalem Delivered*, and *The Faerie Queene*, see my "Lousse and Molloy: Beckett's Bower of Bliss," *Australian Journal of French Studies*, 6 (1969), 65-81.

[3] The translation of "une chemise étrangère" (65) by "another *man's* [my italics] nightgown" and the subsequent contrast and echo in the juxtaposition man-woman make the English text more am-

Like Circe and the potion she employs to turn Ulysses' crewmen into swine, Lousse feeds Molloy her "moly" in order to turn him into a dog: that is, to soften his resistance to her and have him stay as a replacement for Teddy (according to Homer, Hermes gave Ulysses a root called *molü* to protect him against Circe's magic potion): "... doubtless she had poisoned my beer with something intended to mollify me, to mollify Molloy, with the result that I was nothing more than a lump of melting wax, so to speak" (47). The repetition of "mollify" juxtaposed with the name Molloy constitutes an obvious play on words, for Molloy's name is no doubt derived from the Latin *mollis* ("soft" or "pliable"). To this play on words we can add "moly," which, though etymologically unrelated to "mollify" and Molloy, repeats the root *mol*. The notion of softness is further reinforced by the image of the melting wax. Lousse's "moly" will produce the desired effect, but only, as Molloy's surprise indicates, because it brings out within the one who consumes it a penchant for inertia and passivity.

Recalling his temptation to sink into the soft soil of the ditch, Molloy takes this penchant to its ultimate conclusion by merging with the life of Lousse's garden. In true Cartesian fashion, Molloy maintains his autonomous existence by continuing to think. The mental realm — "which [knows] neither seasons nor gardens" (49) — is not governed by the natural processes which organize life in the macrocosm. But somehow Molloy abandons consciousness and permits his mind to break open and be invaded by the garden. Thus Molloy as an individual would "die," but his substance would endure, forever preserved, according to the law of conservation of matter, in the cyclical growth pattern of the garden. [4] Molloy rejects this sort of immortality

---

biguous than the French as to the nature of the garment Molloy finds himself wearing.

[4] The life of the garden seems also to capture Molloy's bicycle, whose disintegration will provide it with additional fertilizer. It is discovered "half buried in a soft bush" (46). In the French the garden assumes an active role, and the word "mollesse" explicitly

because it means remaining eternally trapped in the temporality of the macrocosm: "Yes there were times when I forgot not only who I was, but that I was, forgot to be. Then I was no longer that sealed jar to which I owed my being so well preserved, but a wall gave way and I filled with roots and tame stems for example, stakes long since dead and ready for burning, the recess of night and the imminence of dawn, and then the labour of the planet rolling eager into winter, winter would rid it of these contemptible scabs. Or of that winter I was the precarious calm, the thaw of the snows which make no difference and all the horrors of it all all over again" (49).

Unlike Ulysses, Molloy does not make love to his Circe. Yet during his stay with Lousse he remembers the affair he had with Edith, an old hag like Lousse or like Mag. Beneath the grotesque comedy of their sexual relations lies a more serious view of woman and of love. Edith too extends a soft trap to Molloy. She is Woman the temptress whose pliant flesh threatens Molloy with passivity and absorption. At stake is Molloy's liberty and his very substance, for the inertia of easy eroticism signifies an imprisonment in the body and its desires. Although Molloy contributes to his own ensnarement by massaging his mistress' "rump" with wintergreen, Edith's age and infirmity cause her to die before she can truly cannibalize her lover. The circumstances of her death are in keeping with her role: "She died taking a warm tub, as her custom was before receiving me. It limbered her up" (58). [5]

Edith was of course too old to bear children. But sexual relations may lead to another sort of absorption, analogous to Molloy's merging with the growth of Lousse's garden — self-perpetuation from one generation to the next. Molloy rejects his own birth — the event that both continues and

---

associates the fate of Molloy's bicycle with the name of its owner and the other images of softening in Molloy's part of the novel — "appuyée contre un buisson d'une grande mollesse qui en mangeait la moitié" (69).

[5] "Limber her up" loses the suggestiveness of "cela la ramollissait" (86), where once again the stem *mou/mol* appears.

begins anew the horrors of existence in time — as the "first taste of the shit" (16) but is himself guilty of helping bring someone into the world. He has a son somewhere, the result of a liaison with a chambermaid, an affair he would like to forget: "Don't talk to me about the chambermaid, I should never have mentioned her, she was long before [his affair with Edith], I was sick, perhaps there was no chambermaid, ever, in my life. Molloy, or life without a chambermaid" (58-59).

The imagery of softness has far different connotations in the context of the relationship between Moran and his son. When Moran forces his son to walk in front of him, the sight of the boy's body reminds him that however tyrannical and authoritarian he may be, he cannot transform Moran *fils* into a duplicate of himself: "But apart from having other parts to play during this expedition, than those of keeper and sick-nurse, the prospect was more than I could bear of being unable to move a step without having before my eyes my son's little sullen plump body" (129). Moran's irritation is provoked by the very nature of his son's flesh. "Plump" — reinforced by "sullen" — suggests softness and pliability, an amorphous material that will yield but will not hold its form. Moran sees in his son's body an image of the boy's essential freedom as a subjective Other. Moran *fils* may obey his father's whims — he has little choice — but nonetheless, even before he abandons his father, he plainly represents an element in Moran's well-regulated existence that Moran cannot truly control.

There is another, and more fundamental, soft aspect of Moran's life that escapes his control — Molloy, his emerging antithetical self. Hitherto, Moran's world has been predicated upon neat categories and definitions. It is a world of sharp contours, where things and people are identifiable and sure. As the Molloy element within him manifests itself, those definitions become increasingly blurred, and reality becomes increasingly amorphous, unintelligible, and disturbing.

We have already noted the significance of Molloy's name. Moran is also concerned with Molloy's name: "Of these two names, Molloy and Mollose the second seemed to me perhaps more correct. But barely. What I hear, in my soul I suppose, where the acoustics are so bad, was a first syllable, Mol, very clear, followed almost at once by a second, very thick, as though gobbled by the first, and which might have been oy as it might have been ose, or one, or even oc" (112). The part of the name that Moran hears distinctly is its stem "Mol," which devours with its softness the suffixes that would particularize it. What remains is the undefinable essence of the name, the undefinable self that Molloy attempts to circumscribe and Moran sets out to capture.

Thus the process of "ageing" that Moran undergoes is more than a matter of an excavation toward a deeper level of the mind. It is a process of softening as well. The "prey" that emerges from the block in which it has been imprisoned is, analogous to the name assigned to it, a vague, unidentifiable figure: "But what words can describe this sensation at first all darkness and bulk, with a noise like a grinding of stones, then suddenly as soft as water flowing. And then I saw a little globe swaying up slowly from the depths, through the quiet water, smooth at first, and scarcely paler than its escorting ripples, then little by little a face, with holes for the eyes and mouth and other wounds, and nothing to show if it was a man's face or a woman's face, a young face or an old face, or if its calm too was not an effect of the water trembling between it and the light" (148-149).

Molloy's soft presence disturbs Moran's existence in more oblique ways as well, notably in the quality of the meals Moran eats — or attempts to eat — on the day of Gaber's arrival. Suddenly familiar foods become disgustingly gelatinous or reach some in-between state that is neither solid nor liquid. They revolt Moran, and his inability to recognize them makes him apprehensive. You are what you eat; and, plainly, the nature of the spoiled dishes, their number, and the "coincidence" of their appearance with the announcement of Youdi's order adumbrate the

transformation of Moran himself. He is being given a taste
— quite literally — of a new reality.

Moran's favorite dishes are Irish stew and shepherd's
pie, which even under "normal" conditions are somewhat
soft and amorphous — spoiled, they become even more so. [6]
The Irish stew is a "great disappointment" (102), for it
has been overcooked. The stew's essential ingredient, its
onions, have mingled with the rest to produce a gelatinous
concoction that puzzles and angers Moran: "Where are the
onions? I cried. Gone to nothing, replied Martha. I rushed
into the kitchen, to look for the onions I suspected her of
having removed from the pot, because she knew how much
I liked them. I even rummaged in the bin. Nothing. She
watched me mockingly" (102). At dinner time Moran discovers that his shepherd's pie has met much the same fate
as his Irish stew, and it makes him think of excrement:
"It was while examining the shepherd's pie more narrowly
that I had this afterthought. I lifted the crust with my
spoon and looked inside. I probed it with my fork. I called
Martha and said, His dog wouldn't touch it" (118).

Similarly, Moran's evening soup begins to "coagulate,"
attaining a perplexing undefinable consistency: "Tell me,
Martha, I said, what is this preparation? She named it.
Have I had it before? I said. She assured me I had" (116).
Even the bowl of milk that Moran brings up to his son
(and eventually forces him to drink) does not escape the
"contamination" of the foods with which Moran comes into
contact: "The bowl of milk was growing cold and forming
a revolting skin" (120).

In light of the changes in the quality of Moran's existence, the contrast between the names Molloy and Moran
becomes highly significant. Dropping the suffixes, we can
oppose, following the analysis of Ruby Cohn, [7] the soft,

---

[6] Niklaus Gessner calls Moran's Irish stew a "Sinnbild des Un-
gegliederten im Bereich des Kulinarischen." *Die Unzulänglichkeit
der Sprache: Eine Untersuchung über Formzerfall und Beziehungslosigkeit bei Samuel Beckett* (Zurich: Juris Verlag, 1957), p. 39.

[7] Ruby Cohn, *Samuel Beckett: The Comic Gamut* (New Brunswick, New Jersey: Rutgers University Press, 1962), p. 131.

liquid *l* of Mol to the harder *r* of Mor. As Moran comes to resemble Molloy, the *r* will be devoured by and merge with the *l*.

Despite his name and the quality of his existence, Molloy carries on his person like a talisman a small sucking stone. He is very particular about its nature, preferring the type of stone to be found on the beach, one made smooth and round by the action of the elements and the pounding of the sea. Whereas it is true that sucking upon a small stone can reduce the pangs of hunger and thirst, Molloy's stone is more than a means of assuaging the needs of his body. He clings to it because its nature symbolizes a way of being in the world; it is a vestige of a mode of existence that Molloy has left behind him. Unlike Molloy's body, his bicycle, or his sense of identity, the stone, still full and solid, has triumphed over the forces of disintegration. It is an image of will, certitude, and clarity, in its way a souvenir of better days like Molloy's bicycle horn. Thus when Molloy appeases his appetite with his stone he also appropriates its attributes to himself through its contact with his mouth: "I thought of the food I had refused. I took a pebble from my pocket and sucked it. It was smooth, from having been sucked so long by me and beaten by the storm. A little pebble in your mouth, round and smooth, appeases, soothes, makes you forget your hunger, forget your thirst" (26).

Moran finds an analogous reassurance in things that are hard, smooth, and well defined. His fabricated image of himself contrasts with the self he harbors within the recesses of his mind: "How little one is at one with oneself, good God. I who prided myself on being a sensible man, cold as crystal and as free from spurious depths" (113). Still clinging to this specious self, Moran finds relief from the disquieting events that attend Gaber's visit by gazing upon the hard and smooth fixtures of his bathroom: "What a day.... I sat down on the edge of the bath. The porcelain, the mirrors, the chromium, instilled a great peace within me" (118). Similarly, Moran enjoys "skinning branches and laying bare the pretty white glossy sapwood" (149-150). Ironically, it is with a fire poker made in this fashion that Moran will kill his hulking double and in so doing symbolically shatter the crystalline image he once projected of himself.

III

Sapo does not encounter the same sort of viscous landscape that Molloy does. But nonetheless his movements are "those of one floundering in a quag" (204). Beckett suggests here that Sapo's peculiar way of walking is due to his desire to sink into the earth and thus escape the forces that compel him to move. Sapo's desire reappears in Macmann's story, where it undergoes considerable amplification. Stretched out upon the muddy ground, Macmann becomes literally "of the earth earthy" (243),[8] merging with the landscape, which seems to absorb Macmann's hair and thus Macmann himself: ". . . the rain glued it to the ground and churned it up with the earth and grass into a kind of muddy pulp . . ." (242). Yet even when the ground is dry, Macmann mingles with the landscape. Just as Molloy in his ditch wove the grass around his face and even ate some of it, "on a dry and windy day [Macmann's hair] would have gone romping in the grass almost like grass itself" (242).

Molloy had his Edith; Macmann has Moll. Moll's name suggests softness, and indeed her most conspicuous feature is her soft lips, "so broad and thick that they seemed to devour half the face" (257). At first Macmann resists Moll's advances, but he finally yields to temptation and becomes a captive of those devouring lips: "Inauspicious beginnings indeed, during which his feeling for Moll was frankly one of repugnance. Her lips in particular repelled him, those selfsame lips, or so little changed as to make no matter, that some months later he was to suck with grunts of pleasure, so that at the very sight of them he not only closed his eyes, but covered them with his hands for

---

[8] The repetition of the word "earth" preserves the structure and significance of the French "terre à terre" (129).

greater safety" (263). Though himself a prisoner of love, Macmann grows aware of the appropriative nature of his relationship with Moll, aware that she has ensnared him like bird-lime snares a bird and rendered him powerless. Moll's appearance in his life has destroyed, at least provisionally, the ataraxia he sought in the asylum whose purpose was to "postpone as long as possible the fatal hour" (245). Macmann discovers that love and sex bind him to the external world and only accentuate the ravages of temporality. Thus Moll becomes "Sucky Molly" (262), for she engulfs Macmann, exhausting him and draining his substance. [9] Consequently, Macmann speaks of love as a "lethal glue" (267) and in one of the poems he writes to his mistress he portrays himself and Moll walking hand in hand to the cemetery, equating love with death and burial:

> To the lifelong promised land
> Of the nearest cemetery
> With his Sucky hand in hand
> Love it is at last leads Hairy. (262)

Macmann is delivered from the clutches of love, as was Molloy, through the timely death of his mistress. The circumstances of Moll's death are no less significant and ironic than Edith's. Beckett employs the repulsive spectacle of a malodorous old hag vomiting abundantly to once more depreciate love and sex as leading to procreation. Thus the wasting illness to which Moll succombs bears a resemblance to morning sickness: "Half a century younger she might have been taken for pregnant" (265).

Given the relationship between Malone and Molloy, it is not surprising that Malone numbers a small stone among his possessions. Though he never describes its nature, we

---

[9] In French Moll is called "Poupée Pompette" (167). "Pompette" is the colloquial word for "drunk," and indeed Moll and Macmann are "drunk" on the wine of love. It also suggests the verb *pomper*, which signifies "to pump" or "to suck" and whose past participle *pompé* is the familiar term for "exhausted" or "washed out." True to her name, Moll "exhausts" Macmann, "sucking" away his substance with her soft, devouring lips.

may assume it resembles Molloy's. However, despite the suggested similarities between Malone's period as a wanderer and Molloy's voyage, their relationships with small, hard objects differ. Malone does not limit his interest to small stones but picks up in his travels a variety of objects, a chestnut, a pipe stem, a pine cone, among others. As in the case of Molloy, he is attracted by their compactness and their hard, well-defined contours — though, obviously, they are not necessarily smooth and round. It is through his fingertips that Malone draws stability and reassurance from them; their attributes are opposed to the inexorable blurring of his identity and the dissolution of his body: "... I loved to finger and caress the hard shapely objects that were there in my deep pockets ..." (248). Malone also uses these objects to overcome the limpness of his body during sleep, a limpness which, like Molloy's "stasis" on his bicycle, indicates the eventual triumph of decay and entropy: "And I loved to fall asleep holding in my hand a stone, a horse chestnut or a cone, and I would still be holding it when I woke, my fingers closed over it, in spite of sleep, which makes a rag of the body so it may rest" (248).

Malone the narrator encounters yet another sort of opposition between hardness and softness. He is swept by feelings of one quality or the other, in a process that is interwoven with the expansion and contraction he undergoes as he narrates his stories: "But I have felt so many strange things, so many baseless things assuredly, that they are perhaps better left unsaid. To speak for example of the times when I go liquid and become like mud, what good would that do? Or of the others when I would be lost in the eye of a needle, I am so hard and contracted?" (224-225). The viscous landscape has here been replaced by the verbal mud which, like the primal ooze from which life springs, is the material from which Malone fashions his creations. Analogously, hardness becomes by comparison the attribute of ideal existence through self-realization, the escape from the mire of language that Malone is approaching as he "withers" toward the vanishing point.

IV

The Unnamable finds himself trapped in the viscous grip of language, absorbed in Malone's verbal mud. Thus at one stage of the reduction of his body, the Unnamable compares himself to an egg. He conceives of the latter not only in terms of a spatial configuration but also with reference to the sticky fluid with which an egg is filled. Moreover, an egg is a reproductive body from which new life hatches. For the Unnamable the new life suggested by the image of the egg will be that of his "vice-existers" whose creation will attest to the Unnamable's inability to escape the glue of language: "...I would gladly give myself the shape if not the consistency of an egg ... for the consistency is more like mucilage" (305).

Worm's "birth" illustrates the Unnamable's plight. It is attended by a specious calm. "Apart from the discourse, not a breath" (364), the narrator ironically remarks. The "discourse" refers to the voices of the "delegates" to whom Worm's creation is attributed. The "breath" recalls the verses of Genesis that describe how God created man by breathing into a handful of dust. But unlike Adam, Worm is portrayed as "rooted" in "molasses" or "slime" (364). As a fiction he is mired in spatio-temporel existence no different from the Unnamable.

The same Biblical allusion appears in the Unnamable's depiction of himself. He sees himself caught up in a dust storm of sorts: "...all that is needed is to wander and let wander, be this slow boundless whirlwind and every particle of its dust..." (401). This "whirlwind" is composed of the words in which the Unnamable is dispersed and from which his fictions are born: "...I'm all these words, all these strangers, this dust of words..." (386). But as the victim of language, the Unnamable associates the act of creation with being trapped, like Worm, in disgusting, viscous slime. Hence the Unnamable imagines it has rained and his dust of words has been transformed into imprisoning mud: "...I've always been here, here there was never anyone but me, never, always me, no one, old slush to be churned everlastingly, now it's slush, a minute ago it was dust ..." (403). [10]

Like Malone, the Unnamable "liquifies" into mud and, as in the case of Malone, his imagination turns to the opposing quality of hardness when he describes the characteristics of the ideal mode of existence to which he aspires. He wishes to be "round and hard" (306), a "wordless thing in an empty place, a hard shut dry cold black place" (386).

V

The viscous landscapes into which Molloy and Moran imagine themselves engulfed initiate us into the trilogy's world of mud. In it we witness the blurring of definitions and categories. Identity becomes increasingly amorphous and difficult to define. The Other, in the form of Woman, is revealed to be a soft, sticky snare that threatens to absorb the hero. Moll is the surpreme temptress of the trilogy; her lips profer sensual delight as they secrete the lethal glue of temporality.

In a world gone soft, the hard, indestructible object, carried on one's person like a charm, transmits its magical reassurance and certainty. Its hardness becomes the quality of selfhood, the attainment of which signifies the transcendance of viscous existence.

Yet as the trilogy concludes, the protagonist is left trapped in the slime of literary creation. Unable to define the self, the Unnamable remains entombed in a hell not unlike that of the sullen imprisoned under the mud in Dante's *Inferno*. Like them, the Unnamable is condemned to babble his strange litany as his every attempt to find a name for himself causes yet another fiction to grow out of the inexhaustible verbal ooze.

---

[10] The English "slush" loses the immediate connotations of mud and putrefaction present in the French "fange" (238). Beckett had previously translated "fange" (158) as "slime" (364) when he described how Worm was mired in language.

CHAPTER IV

LIGHT FALLS

I

ONE OF THE MOST conspicuous features of the landscapes of
the trilogy, be it the landscape of external reality or the
inner landscape from which the author-protagonist unravels
his tale, is their light. Molloy and Moran reside in regions
not unlike Beckett's native Ireland: there are brief periods
of sunlight during the day, but most of the time a rainy
mist darkens the sky. Within the purgatorial internal landscape, the light is crepuscular. This is the gray zone that
Molloy, Malone, and the Unnamable come to inhabit and
from which they long to escape.

Beckett's protagonists sometimes are attracted to light,
but most often it is darkness they seek. Light and dark
are, of course, traditionally symbolic of antithetical aspects
of human existence: comprehension, order, and harmony
as opposed to confusion, chaos, and despair. Within the
trilogy, however, the play between light and dark is considerably more complex than this symbolism might indicate. Beckett reverses the values attached to light and
dark while at the same time maintaining their usual significance. We shall see how Beckett achieves this in his
use of the opposition between light and dark to contrast
inauthentic and authentic existence, macrocosm and microcosm, fiction and the self.

II

In his mother's room, Molloy's vision is growing fee-
bler: "All grows dim. A little more and you'll go blind" (8).
Molloy's failing eyesight signifies more than just the decline
of another part of his sensory apparatus. When he thinks of
the "light of other days" it is "without regret" (8) because he has journeyed to his mother's room to become
"blind": that is to say, he wishes to leave the macrocosm,
associated with light, so that he may accede to the absolute
darkness of the self. In Beckett's cosmology the divine light
of paradise has been replaced by total absence of light.

But Molloy has not reached the darkness he seeks. He
is on the brink of the void in a "no man's land, lying somewhere between existence in time and life in eternity, neither
one nor the other but with characteristics of each." [1] Thus
the light of Molloy's inner space is a half light, "a faint
untroubled sky, enough to see by" (40). This light will not
be extinguished until Molloy finds the words that will
permit him to cross the threshold of the void. Attaining the
darkness he seeks becomes analogous to reaching the center
of the circle, and Molloy depicts his inner light as "yielding
towards an end it seems can never come" (40).

In order to reach this purgatorial zone, Molloy has had
to travel through the light of external reality. Leaving the
twilight world of his Belacqua-like repose in the shadow
of a boulder, Molloy is compelled to emerge into the light
as he takes up the journey to his mother's room. Molloy,
who despises having been born, describes his native city
as the place where he had first seen the "murk of day"
(31). This inversion of the usual expression "light of
day" reveals the ambivalence of the light imagery used to
characterize Molloy's quest, an ambivalence generated by
Molloy's view of existence and by the nature of the self.
Birth signifies a departure from the comfortable darkness

---

[1] Ross Chambers, "Beckett's Brinkmanship," in *Samuel Beckett: A Collection of Critical Essays*, ed. Martin Esslin (Englewood Cliffs, New Jersey: Spectrum Books, 1965), p. 157.

of the womb, an expulsion into the light of the macrocosm, and an initiation into the "murk" of an existence from which the light of logic and comprehension have been excluded.

Molloy's departure takes place between eleven and twelve o'clock, when the sun has approached its zenith, and during the period of the summer solstice — the time of year when the days are longest. An image of urine translates Molloy's disparagement of this season of sunshine: "... the second or third week of June, at the moment that is to say most painful of all when over what is called our hemisphere the sun is at its pitilessmost and the arctic radiance comes pissing on our midnights" (17). Similarly, Molloy denounces the deleterious effects of sunlight: "... the sun, hoisting itself higher and higher in the east, had poisoned me, while I slept. I ought to have put the bulk of the rock between it and me before closing my eyes" (19). Thus Molloy emerges into the light that heralds a possible rebirth, but, in so doing, he has also opted for the destiny of C, the vagabond whom Molloy observed from the shadow of his rock — "to be abroad, by unknown ways, in the gathering night" (10).

Despite the circumstances attending Molloy's departure, the usual nature of the light in Molloy's region suggests a dying world, one which some day, given the entropy of the universe, will not be resurrected by the dawn: "... the mornings were often sunny, in that part of the world, until ten o'clock or coming up to eleven, and that then the sky darkened and the rain fell, fell till evening. Then the sun came out and went down, the drenched earth sparkled an instant, then went out, bereft of light" (30). The moment of the sky's "winding" in the "shroud" of night is described in detail by the narrator: "... there a pale and dying sky, and the sun, already down, was manifest in the living tongue of fire darting towards the zenith, falling and darting again, ever more pale and languid, and doomed no sooner lit to be extinguished" (65).

The "dying sun" to which Molloy awakens causes him to make a significant "error" in navigation. When he leaves

Lousse's city, he decides to travel towards the east, taking the direction of the sun to guide him. However, the sun he sees is not that of the dawn appearing in the east but the setting sun extinguishing itself in the west. In terms of the traditional symbolism of dawn and twilight, Molloy would be traveling toward death. But within the context of Molloy's quest, the direction he takes signifies rebirth, for only by dying to external reality can he achieve his goal.

The rain that falls in Molloy's region and obscures its light is, analogous to the light itself, a correlative of Molloy's situation: "When I wake I see the first things quite clearly, the first things that offer, and I understand them, when they are not too difficult. Then in my eyes and in my head a fine rain begins to fall . . ." (28). The effect of this mist is to becloud external reality and, in so doing, obscure Molloy's sense of identity, structured through his relationships with that reality. The pursuit of his quest is, of course, concomitant with the dissolution of his identity: ". . . that mist . . . which rises in me every day and veils the world from me and veils me from myself" (29). Molloy welcomes the gloom that envelops him, for it is a reflection of his own nature: "The Aegean, thirsting for heat and light, him I killed, he killed himself, early on, in me. The pale gloom of rainy days was better fitted to my taste, no, that's not it, to my humour, no, that's not it either, I had neither taste nor humour, I lost them early on. Perhaps what I mean is that the pale gloom, etc. hid me better, without its being on that account particularly pleasing to me. Chameleon in spite of himself, there you have Molloy, viewed from a certain angle" (30).

During the course of his journey, Molloy has a number of encounters with society. The first of these contacts takes place in the town in which Molloy is arrested. Once he has relinquished his "raglimp stasis" Molloy no longer poses an immediate threat to the self-delusion of the citizenry, and his first few hours in the town are bathed in sunlight, a light that is a correlative of the peace and harmony Molloy sees around him. It is around noon as Molloy, accompanied by a policeman, passes through the "quiet sunlit streets"

(20). The townspeople resting in the warm sunshine observe them serenely: "It was the hour of rest, the forenoon's toil ended, the afternoon's to come. The wisest perhaps, lying in the squares or sitting on their door-steps, were savouring its languid ending, forgetful of recent cares, indifferent to those at hand" (21).

Molloy too forgets his cares and yields to this moment of peace. He has come out of the darkness of solitude and alienation and, for a brief time at least, will participate in the order of society. Through his arrest he has become a ward of society, and his activities now fall within its structures and institutions. Thus society can assume responsibility for Molloy's existence and give it meaning within its framework — freeing Molloy from the burden of seeking self-definition by means of his journey to his mother's room: "While still putting my best foot foremost, I gave myself up to that golden moment, as if I had been someone else.... Forgetful of my mother, set free from the act, merged in this alien hour, saying, Respite, respite" (21).

Molloy's surrender to this sunlit moment of tranquility, as if he were another, indicates that at one time he was indeed another — no different from the townspeople who watch him go by. Thus the light that illuminates his passage through the streets is associated with a former mode of existence. This identification is reinforced by Molloy's experience in the police commissioner's office. There, the light streaming through the window rescussitates within him the desire to sit down (an act which he can now perform only with great difficulty) and brings forth his name. Both these effects of the sunlight reveal Molloy's temporary reintegration into society; he has the desires and identity that any man might have: "And yet the desire to sit down came upon me from time from time to time, back upon me from a vanished world. And I did not always resist it, forewarned though I was. Yes, my mind felt it surely, this tiny sediment, incomprehensibly stirring like grit at the bottom of a puddle, while on my face and great big Adam's apple the air of summer weighed and the splendid summer sky. And suddenly I remembered my name, Molloy" (22-23).

Molloy's moment in the sun is, as he himself indicates, a passing illusion. The law which once enfolded him in its order manifests its mystery and unintelligibility. And if this is the nature of the law, then the harmony of the society based upon it can only be a veneer. Thus the light of the commissioner's office yields to the darkness of the guard-room filled with shadowy forms: "The room was dark and full of people hastening to and fro, malefactors, policemen, lawyers, priests and journalists I suppose. All that made a dark, dark forms crowding in a dark place" (23).

The setting sun marks Molloy's departure from the town and the end of his "golden moment." As a parting gesture, Molloy amuses himself with the shadow he casts on the wall of the police station. He plays at leaving on his bi-cycle, as if to test the reactions of those who observe this spectacle, hoping for a sign that will encourage him to stay and quite certain it will not come. Molloy provokes only laughter or indifference, and thus, reduced once more to a shadow, to the stranger he had been, he resumes his quest

> ... the declining sun fell full on the the white wall of the barracks.... A confused shadow was cast. It was I and my bicycle. I began to play, gesticulating, waving my hat, moving my bicycle to and fro be-fore me, blowing the horn, watching the wall. They were watching me through the bars, I felt their eyes upon me. The policeman on guard at the door told me to go away. He needn't have, I was calm again. The shadow in the end is no better than the substance. I asked the man to help me, to have pity on me. He didn't understand.... The man came towards me, angered by my slowness. Him too they were watching, through the windows. Somewhere someone laughed. Inside me too someone was laugh-ing. I took my sick leg in my hands and passed it over the frame. I went. (25-26)

Molloy's subsequent contacts with society will be mark-ed by hostility and thus by an absence of light. When

Molloy is threatened by an enraged mob after he runs over Teddy, he rejects being "abroad" and "visible" (35) and takes refuge with Lousse. Later, Molloy, the misfit and pariah, becomes the prey of society, organized into teams of exterminators. Light is now associated with persecution and death, for the exterminators are most active during the daylight hours:

> They wake up, hale and hearty, their tongues hanging out for order, beauty and justice, baying for their due. Yes, from eight or nine till noon is the dangerous time. But towards noon things quiet down, the most implacable are sated, they go home, it might have been better but they've done a good job, there have been a few survivors but they'll give no more trouble, each man counts his rats. It may begin again in the early afternoon ... but it's nothing compared to the morning, mere fun. Coming up to four or five of course there is the nightshift, the watchmen, beginning to bestir themselves. . . . the night purge is in the hands of technicians, for the most part. They do nothing else, the bulk of the population have no part in it, preferring their warm beds. . . . Day is the time for lynching. . . . (67)

Forced to hide during the day, Molloy comes alive with nightfall, like C. Once more he is the "chameleon," the incarnation of the dark side of existence, the side that those who live in the light cannot see or hide from themselves: "But already the day is over, the shadows lengthen, the walls multiply, you hug the walls. . . . Then the true night, perilous too but sweet to him who knows it, who can open to it like the flower to the sun, who himself is night, day and night" (67).

The last stages of Molloy's journey reveal yet another play between light and dark. The forest with its dense vegetation enshrouds him in its protective darkness, and Molloy is careful to avoid those areas where too much light penetrates: "Here the gloom was not so thick and I made haste to leave it. I don't like gloom to lighten, there's something shady about it" (83). What is most "shady" about the

gloom is that Molloy must eventually leave it behind. Just
as Molloy was obliged to leave the shadow of the boulder
and emerge into the light, so too, compelled by his imperative, he will be forced to foresake the woods and enter
into the light that once again separates him from his
mother's room and its promise of endless night: "And yet
I did not despair of seeing the light tremble, some day,
through the still boughs, the strange light of the plain, its
pale wild eddies, through the bronze-still boughs, which no
breath ever stirred. But it was a day I dreaded too. So that
I was sure it would come sooner or later. For it was not
bad being in the forest, I could imagine worse, and I could
have stayed there till I died, unrepining, yes, without pining
for the light . . ." (86).

Just as Gaber's arrival shattered the stillness of Moran's
tranquil Sunday morning, analogously it will cast his existence into darkness. That is to say, Moran, like Molloy,
will be compelled to pass through the light, and thus the
gloom, of existence in order to reach the paradise of rebirth
in the darkness of the void. Hitherto, Moran had been a
"contrivance" turned toward the light of the outside world
in which he constituted his identity — "creature of his
house, of his garden, of his few poor possessions, discharg-
ing faithfully and ably a revolting function, reining back
his thoughts within the limits of the calculable . . ." (114).

But when Moran foresakes the external landscape for
the internal one, he passes judgement upon existence in the
macrocosm and upon his fabricated identity. He rejects its
"dingy light" for the darkness of his mind. Finding Molloy
is, of course, the key to attaining the deepest level of consciousness and absolute darkness. But Moran begins his
quest with a notion of his quarry no less contrived than
Moran himself. This conceptualized Molloy is the one
"brought to light that memorable August Sunday" and
contrasts with the real Molloy, the "true denizen" of
Moran's "dark places" (114).

In our present context the crucial passages describing Moran's "ageing" are once again essential to our understanding of the relationship between Moran and his

antithetical self. The transformation of Moran's inner landscape signifies a penetration of its darkness — "a kind of
clawing toward a light and countenance I could not name"
(148). We have already identified that face "swaying up
slowly from the depths" (148) with Molloy. Here the play
between light and dark leads to a reversal of their usual
associations. Light is indeed symbolic of birth, but the face
that emerges from Moran's depths marks the destruction of
Moran's fabricated self and hence both casts a pall over the
light to which Moran was once turned and points the way
toward the darkness of the void where Moran may be
reborn. Unlike the old Moran, who would have attempted
to find some explanation for his unsettling experience, the
new Moran is indifferent to what has taken place. Aware
that his sense of identity — once so clear — has become as
obscure as the shadows that now envelope him, he foresakes enlightenment: "But at the first faint light, I mean
in these wild shadows gathering about me, dispensed by a
vision or by an effort of thought, at the first light I fled
to other cares. . . . And he who acted thus was a stranger to
me too" (149).

A parallel and equally complex opposition between light
and dark characterizes the two encounters that take place
at Moran's camp site. The first passerby — the vagabond
who resembles C and Molloy — fascinates Moran with his
"pale and noble face" (146), which Moran envies; his manner of speaking, as if he were a foreigner or "had lost the
habit of speech" (146); and his staff, which Moran hefts
in his hand. Moran would like to shed some light, literally
and figuratively, on this intriguing figure: "He threw me a
last look and went. It was almost dark. He walked with
a swift uncertain step, often changing his course, dragging
his stick like a hindrance. I wished I could have stood
there looking after him, and time at a standstill. I wished
I could have been in the middle of a desert, under the mid-
day sun, to look after him till he was only a dot, on the
edge of the horizon" (146-147).

Yet despite his interest in this vagabond, a curiosity
provoked by the man's resemblance to Moran's quarry,

Moran lets him go without making any effort to retain him and without asking him any questions. As a surrogate for Molloy, his disappearance into the darkness parallels that of Moran's apparition into the "wild shadows." In both cases Moran seems to resign himself to the futility of trying to comprehend the mysteries that have entered his life and accepts the darkness he once denied.

The second stranger contrasts sharply with the man he is pursuing. He provokes feelings of disgust and fear in Moran, whom he resembles: "... the face ... I regret to say vaguely resembled my own, less the refinement of course, same little abortive moustache, same little ferrety eyes, same paraphimosis of the nose, and a thin red mouth that looked as if it was raw from trying to shit its tongue" (151). These antipathetical aspects are heightened and reinforced by the dark clothing in which the stranger is enveloped, clothing that gives him a hulking, menacing look. His appearance is analogous to the sensation of "darkness and bulk" that gives way during Moran's "ageing": "He was on the small side, but thick-set. He wore a thick navy-blue suit ... of hideous cut and a pair of outrageously wide black shoes.... The fringed extremities of a dark muffler, seven feet long at least, wound several times round his neck, hung down his back" (150). And the stranger's death results in a similar liberation. When Moran examines the corpse, he notes, "he no longer resembled me" (151). Thus Moran has destroyed his dark double, a destruction we can equate with the collapse of Moran's contrived self; and in so doing he has freed the first passerby from his pursuer, just as the long-denied countenace was freed from its prison. As in the instance of his "ageing," Moran has lost the specious light (hence the dark stranger) of a fabricated identity in order that he may become an unidentifiable figure moving along the path that leads to the ultimate darkness.

Although Moran, like a true secret agent, had departed at midnight, he had nonetheless, unlike previous missions, chosen to travel in the light of day in order to cling a little bit longer to the light that he associates with a secure and

comfortable mode of existence: "The right thing would
have been to travel by night and hide during the day, at
least in the early stages. But the weather was so fine I
could not bring myself to do it. My pleasure was not my
sole consideration, but it was a consideration! Such a thing
had never happened to me before, in the course of my
work" (136). The trip home, however, is far from pleasur-
able. Moran's existence has been profoundly transformed,
and the nature of the light in which he travels corresponds
to these changes. It is winter, and the sky is almost continuously obscured by some form of precipitation. When
Moran arrives home he finds his house dark and deserted.
The current has been disconnected by the electrical company, and Moran, having been initiated into the gloom of
existence, does not bother to have it turned back on. But
despite the alterations to his personality, Moran's old self
dies hard. Before departing upon the long and difficult
journey in the shadows that awaits him, Moran allows himself some last moments in the sun — enjoying the "longest,
loveliest days of all the year" (175).

III

Though considerably younger than Moran, like the latter, Sapo is at first turned toward the light. He is eager for
comprehension and self-definition and opposed to those
aspects of existence that are mysterious and puzzling:
"... this patient, reasonable child, struggling all alone for
years to shed a little light upon himself, avid of the least
gleam, a stranger to the joys of darkness" (193). But like
Moran, Sapo too is initiated into the darkness. His ap-
prenticeship takes place in the Lambert kitchen. As in the
case of Moran, light is associated here with the noise and
tumult of the macrocosm — whose sounds come to Sapo
from just beyond the threshold of the darkening room.
Apprehensive about cutting himself off from that familiar
world, Sapo turns from time to time towards the light for
reassurance: "And Sapo, his face turned towards an earth

so resplendent that it hurt his eyes, felt at his back and all about him the unconquerable dark, and it licked the light on his face. Sometimes abruptly he turned to face it, letting it envelop and pervade him, with a kind of relief. Then he heard more clearly the sounds of those at work, the daughter calling to her goats, the father cursing his mule" (203). Yet the shadows that fill the room attract Sapo even more, for their darkness signifies the death of the world outside the kitchen door and a tranquility that is the antithesis of its commotion. Sapo's retreat into the darkness of the kitchen is an analogue for a retreat into the mental realm, into a mode of existence beyond understanding: "But silence was in the heart of the dark, the silence of dust and the things that would never stir, if left alone. And the ticking of the invisible alarmclock was as the voice of that silence which, like the dark, would one day triumph too. And then all would be still and dark, and all things at rest for ever at last" (203).[2]

Malone assigns to Macmann the frozen half-light that illuminates the endless period of waiting: "And perhaps he has come to the stage of his instant when to live is to wander the last, of the living in the depths of an instant without bounds, where the light never changes and the wrecks look all alike" (233). But Macmann never reaches this stage of the journey, as does his creator Malone, of whom he is but a "vice-exister." Instead, we find him confronting a gloom similar to that described by Molloy. His desire to rejoin the world outside the asylum is frustrated by a pall that is a correlative of the suffering and absurdity through which he himself once passed: "The road appeared white with dust, bordered with dark masses, stretched a little way and ran up dead, against a narrow grey sky" (279). There is nothing left for Macmann outside the asylum and nothing left for him within it but exile and solitude;

---

[2] Eugene Webb examines this and other examples of light imagery in *Malone Dies*, but with quite different conclusions. See *Samuel Beckett: A Study of His Novels* (Seattle and London: University of Washington Press, 1970), pp. 121-123.

the asylum has its own darkness: "Little by little the haze formed again, and the sense of absence, and the captive things began to murmur again, each one to itself, and it was as if nothing had ever happened or would ever happen again" (279).

Malone himself has retreated from the light of external reality into his room. But the cycle of day and night, of light and dark, continues to function outside the window of his room. Malone's dawn, like Molloy's, turns out to be twilight. But for Malone this confusion represents a disparity between his temporal situation and the objective time of the universe. As Malone lies dying and narrating, he is approaching the end of time and consequently his time is slowing down. Analogous to Molloy's experience in Lousse's house, the alternation of light and dark outside Malone's window appears accelerated. Dusk follows almost immediately upon dawn with scarcely any daytime to separate them: "But the light, instead of being the dawn, turned out in a very short time to be the dusk. And the sun, instead of rising higher and higher in the sky as I confidently expected, calmly set, and night, the passing of which I had just celebrated after my fashion, calmly fell again" (220). Malone's task will be to eliminate this interval between day and night and bring about unending darkness. In order to do this he must attend to the light of his literary landscape.

As the author of the novels that precede *Malone Dies*, Malone, looking at his writings in retrospect, divides his fictional output into three phases, which parallel the evolution of Beckett's fiction. The first of these corresponds no doubt to the creation of *Murphy* and of *Watt*. This period is associated with light, for in Malone's estimation this sort of literature was relatively facile and free from the ambiguities of his later works: "I turned on all the lights, I took a good look around, I began to play with what I saw. People and things ask nothing better than to play, certain animals too. All went well at first, they all came to me, pleased that someone should want to play with them. If I said, Now I need a hunchback [Hackett?], immediately one came running, proud as punch of his fine hunch that was going to perform" (180). The game, however, became serious — probably because the reality Malone had played with began to crumble away, language and the creation of fiction had become open to doubt, and the self of the author had become involved in his stories. Malone's first "manner" did not fulfill its promises: "But it was not long before I found myself alone in the dark" (180). The second period will thus be characterized by darkness and probably corresponds to the writing of *Mercier et Camier* and the *Stories*: "... I gave up trying to play and took to myself for ever shapelessness and speechlessness, incurious wondering, darkness, long stumbling with outstretched arms, hiding" (180).

In his third period, concomitant with the creation of *Molloy*, Malone accomodated himself to his failure as a writer. The creation of fiction has become a futile quest for the self.[3] Malone — himself a fiction — emerges by means of language into the spatio-temporal world of men, into the "stinging air" (195), knowing he will only fall back into the darkness, into the void of consciousness in which the self resides but, unverbalized, cannot come into being: "... the rapture of vertigo, the letting go, the fall, the gulf, the relapse to darkness, to nothingness ..." (195).[4]

These judgements on the nature of the fictions he has hitherto created constitute Malone's point of departure for his view of the stories he now sets out to write. Once again literature is to be a game, simply a means of killing time. His period of groping for the self — the "long blind road" (182) — is over, he believes; and he intends to resist involving himself in the complexities of "serious" creation and be immune to the lure of the "old fog" (182).

---

[3] Cf. Beckett's esthetic of failure in Samuel Beckett and Georges Duthuit, "Three Dialogues," *Transition 49*, No. 5 (December 1949), p. 103.

[4] In the French the opposition between the light of fiction and the darkness of the self is more sharply delineated. There Malone emerges not into the "stinging air" but into the "lumière cinglante" (137).

When Malone realizes that his initial project is futile, that Sapo-Macmann is a fragment of himself, his reaction is expressed in the imagery of darkness characteristic of the later phases of his writing: "I feel the old dark gathering, the solitude preparing, by which I know myself..." (189). In order to tell Sapo's story after the fashion (ideally) of his first period, he intends to make it a linear progression in which past, present, and future will be linked by a rigorous causality. In order to do so, every aspect of the story must fit a logical pattern with no lacunae — what Beckett called in *Proust* the "vulgarity of a plausible concatenation" (62). Malone loses control of his material when he is unable to explain why Sapo was not expelled from school after throwing an eraser through a closed window. Malone's story impinges upon that of his "invention," and the two do not mesh. The absence of a link may destroy the entire chain:

> ...I must try and discover... why Sapo was not expelled when he so richly deserved to be. For I want as little as possible of darkness in his story. A little darkness, in itself, at the time, is nothing. You think no more about it and you go on. But I know what darkness is, it accumulates, thickens, then suddenly bursts and drowns everything.
>
> ...I shall make him live as though he had been punished according to his deserts. We shall turn our backs on this little cloud, but we shall not let it out of our sight. It will not cover the sky without our knowing, we shall not suddenly raise our eyes, far from help, far from shelter, to a sky black as ink. (190)

Despite the implausibilities of his story and the tedium of attempting to tell it with words that "are no shoddier than what they peddle" (195), Malone must pursue it until the end comes, without "letting go." Similar to the opposition between expansion and contraction, softening and hardening, Malone must move toward the light and toward the darkness simultaneously, exhausting his life in the light through his narration as he himself dies so as to liberate the "stranger" (195) who resides in his dark depths. An examination of the light within Malone's room will permit us to better understand this process.

Concomitant with Malone's purgatorial situation, the light within his room is a "grey incandescence" (221): "...here all bathes, I will not say in shadow, nor even half shadow, but in a kind of leaden light that makes no shadow, so that it is hard to say from what direction it comes, for it seems to come from all directions at once, and with equal force" (220). Malone raises a question here concerning the provenance of the light in his room. It does not come from outside and there is no source of light within the room. Malone himself must therefore be the origin of the light. His creative consciousness illuminates the mental microcosm from which his fictions are projected into the world of sunlight outside the room: "But my fingers ... write in other latitudes.... And perhaps on my hands it is the shimmer of the shadows of leaves and flowers and the brightness of a forgotten sun" (234).

Malone is thus a beacon of language illuminating the darkness with which he hopes to be reunited. This light can be provisionally extinguished. Similar to Molloy's experience in Lousse's garden, when he forgot "to be," Malone can temporarily turn off his consciousness. He then can transcend existence: "And if I close my eyes, close them really, as others cannot, but as I can, for there are limits to my impotence, then sometimes my bed is caught up into the air and tossed like a straw by the swirling eddies, and I in it. Fortunately it is not so much an affair of eyelids, but as it were the soul that must be veiled, that soul denied in vain, vigilant, anxious, turning in its cage as in a lantern, in the night without haven or craft or matter or understanding" (222).

As Malone prepares to embark upon this empty black sea, the grey light of his room brightens, heralding the approaching moment of rebirth: "Leaden light again, thick, eddying, riddled with little tunnels through to brightness.... I am being given, if I may venture the expression, birth to into death, such is my impression" (283). Macmann and Lemuel in their boat are the point of departure for a panoramic night scene that recalls the port of darkness that Malone "saw" when he "closed his eyes" as it scoffs at the light:

> The night is strewn with absurd
> absurd lights, the stars, the beacons, the buoys,
> the lights of earth and in the hills the faint fires
> of the blazing gorse. (287)

A final "never... light" (288) plunges the universe into obscurity. Malone's beacon has flickered and died, but, as we shall see, there still remains a self that must be brought into the light.

IV

"What rubbish all this stuff about light and dark" (306) the Unnamable declares, underlining the role the imagery of light and dark has played in the first two volumes of the trilogy and resigning himself to its perpetuation in the concluding volume. That the Unnamable is not the "stranger" Malone thought he would bring into being is evinced by the continuing presence of light in the Unnamable's space — a grey light similar to the sort that illuminated Malone's room — where there should be only the darkness of the void: "Yes, out with them, there is no light here. No grey either, black is what I should have said. Nothing then but me, of which I know nothing, except that I have never uttered, and this black, of which I know nothing either, except that it is black, and empty" (304).

As it was in *Molloy* and *Malone Dies*, light in *The Unnamable* is associated with the spatio-temporal world of men. Employing an image of urine similar to one used by Molloy when he left the shadow of his boulder, the Unnamable rejects the light and the existence it represents: "... where men come and go ... in the light of a choice of luminaries pissing on the darkness turn about, so that it is never dark, never deserted, that must be terrible" (314-

315). Concomitant with this denigration is the Unnamable's repudiation of the creations by which he was projected into the light: "Why did I have myself represented in the midst of men, the light of day? It seems to me it was none of my doing. We won't go into that now. I can see them still, my delegates. The things they have told me! About men, the light of day" (297).

By assigning to his "delegates" the responsibility for having informed him about the light, the Unnamable makes the "delegates" its source. They are the bearers of the words from which the Unnamable continues to be absent, and their language generates the light. "Is it I who cast the faint light that enables me to see what goes on under my nose?" the Unnamable asks. "There is nothing to be gained, for the moment," he replies, "by supposing so" (300). Thus, unlike Malone, the Unnamable attributes his light to nameless others, and they torture him with their lamps as they torture him with their words.

Unlike Malone's beacon, the lights of the "delegates" shine unevenly. Their flickering may represent the pulsations of the narration, the sputterings of a voice in the dark that, despite its intentions, keeps renewing itself. More likely, it represents the possibility of change. The Unnamable seems to believe for a brief moment that the self can finally be described; and thus the voices and the lights of the "delegates" — who, it must be remembered, are "lies" like everything else in the novel — will be extinguished, leaving the Unnamable to be himself in the silence and the darkness:

> These lights for instance, which I do not require to mean anything, what is there so strange about them, so wrong? Is it their irregularity, their instability, their shining strong one minute and weak the next, but never beyond the power of one or two candles. . . . But the play of the lights is truly unpredictable. . . . I shall remark without further delay, in order to be sure of doing so, that I am relying on these lights . . . to help me continue and perhaps even conclude. (204)

Despite the Unnamable's hopes, nothing changes, and he remains a prisoner of words and of the lights. But in so doing he raises a tantalizing question. A remark he makes, "silence once broken will never again be whole" (366) applies equally to the problem of the lights. Once the self has been exfoliated into time and space there can be no assurance that after these excrescences have been stripped away the same phenomenon will not reoccur. Thus the lights may go out, only to be relit: "... the black proves ... nothing ... as to the nature of the silence which it inspissates (as it were)" (365).

Worm is no less able to flee the light than the Unnamable. Conceived in words, Worm necessarily falls victim to the lights of the "delegates." Like the other protagonists of the trilogy, Worm has his own quest for darkness and his search too only projects him into the light. The "delegates" are thus able to lure Worm into existence with their lamps: "For it is obvious the light would lessen as he went towards it, they would see to that, to make him think he was on the right road and so bring him to the wall. Then the blaze, the capture and the paean" (366).

V

It was Mag, Molloy tells us, who brought him into the night. The light of birth was the beginning of the unending cruelty of temporal existence. Yet men live in a world of light, illuminating the darkness however they can. And within their light is to be found many possibilities of self-definition, in the social and legal structures man establishes to shut out the darkness of chaos and absurdity that, according to Beckett, lie at the heart of life. This is the light in which Molloy permits himself to bask for a moment and toward which Moran and Sapo temporarily turn. Ultimately, that light is revealed to be illusory. The wanderer returns to, or discovers, the darkness of existence in the light, through which he must journey in order to be reborn into the paradise of everlasting darkness.

But the protagonist-narrator terminates his voyage in the grey light of purgatory, where he waits and narrates. "Life up there in the light," spatio-temporal existence, sticks to him like a bur, for it resides in the words he uses. Language thus becomes a beacon that exiles the protagonist from the darkness of the self and lights the literary landscape of his pseudo-selves.

Throughout the trilogy Beckett plays on the traditional values of light and dark. In a larger sense he utilizes the identity of opposites, making the greatest light equal the greatest dark.[5] The effect on the reader is to draw him into a recognizable fable while causing him to experience what David Hayman has termed a "flux of movement in [his] brain."[6] If all literature is "rubbish" as the Unnamable suggests, then, from the same perspective, the light imagery of the trilogy is only another bit of verbal legerdemain. But from the reader's point of view, it constitutes an essential aspect of a unique vision and art.

---

[5] Beckett discussed Giordano Bruno's theory of the identity of opposites in "Dante... Bruno. Vico... Joyce," *Transition 16-17* (June 1929), p. 244. See also Aldo Tagliaferri, "Gli identici contrari e la crisi dell' identità," in *Beckett e l'iperdeterminazione letterarie* (Milan: Feltrinelli, 1967), pp. 27-37.

[6] David Hayman, "Molloy or the Quest for Meaninglessness," in *Samuel Beckett Now*, ed. Melvin J. Friedman (Chicago: University of Chicago Press, 1970), p. 147.

CHAPTER V

A BECKETT BESTIARY

I

BECKETT'S CRITICS HAVE PAID a great deal of attention to the characters of the trilogy but relatively little consideration has been given to its other existants — the animals. Yet animals are present everywhere, crossing the paths of the protagonists or haunting their imaginations. Few wild animals appear in the trilogy; most are the domestic kind: dogs, sheep, horses, asses, chickens, bees, parrots. In a third category are the vermin, rats and flies; they too exist in close association with men.

These animals are, as we shall see, not merely ornamental. Their fate and their characteristics reflect back upon the humans in whose lives they participate. An examination of their role affords us as well a special insight into Beckett's sensitivity.

II

Molloy reacts strongly when he observes A seizing hold of a constipated stray pomeranian that seems to have been following him. Molloy's description of the incident reveals both a sympathy for the plight of the wanderer and a hostility toward the individual who victimizes a helpless dog and uses it as an "ersatz love": [1]

---

[1] Huguette Delye, *Samuel Beckett, ou la philosophie de l'absurde* (Aix-en-Provence: Publications des Annales de la Faculté des Lettres, Aix-en-Provence, 1960), p. 92.

... and what prevented the dog from being one of those stray dogs that you pick up and take in your arms, from compassion or because you have long been straying with no other company than the endless roads, shingle, bogs and heather, than this nature answerable to another court, than at long intervals the fellow-convict you long to stop, embrace, suck, suckle and whom you pass by, with hostile eyes, for fear of his familiarities? Until the day when, your endurance gone in this world for you without arms, you catch up in yours the first mangy cur you meet, carry it the time needed for it to love you and you it, then throw it away. Perhaps he had come to that, in spite of appearances. (12)

A second dog victim appears when Molloy inadvertently runs over Lousse's Teddy. We have already identified Lousse with Circe. In our present context she can be identified with Hecate as well — the crone who was the goddess of the underworld and a practitioner of magic. Her emblem was the dog and she was thus sometimes depicted as a bitch. In Rome dogs were sacrificed to this "beautiful, fecund, devouring mother: life-giving, life-taking." [2] Teddy was about to be sacrificed to Lousse's indifference, for when Molloy ran him down she was on the way to the veterinarian's to have the dog put to sleep. Although Lousse had loved Teddy "like her own child" (33), it had become, like Lousse and Molloy, a victim of time's destruction — "old, blind, deaf, crippled with rheumatism and perpetually incontinent, night and day, indoors and out of doors" (33). He smells of the gangrene of time, "like an old dog, not like a dead dog" (36). A captive in life, Teddy is one in death as well, for he is buried with his leash and collar. At Lousse's house, Molloy's fate is equated with the life and death of this old dog. He will be used by Lousse just as she used Teddy and A his pomeranian: "I would as it were take the place of the dog I had killed, as it for her had taken the place of the child" (46).

---

[2] Maria Leach, *God Had A Dog* (New Brunswick, New Jersey: Rutgers University Press, 1961), p. 21.

The dog's life Molloy assumes at Lousse's house is more than the result of a temporary imprisonment. It cristallizes a fundamental aspect of his existence, one that Molloy inherited at birth. Molloy's description of his mother suggests a dog. Using an epithet one would apply to an animal, he calls Mag "uniparous," "a poor old uniparous whore" (19). Having subjected Mag to a long "period of training" (18), Molloy communicates with his mother by striking her on the head, as he might do with a dumb animal. Mag smells her offspring when he enters her room — "she knew it was me by my odor" (17). The dog image is reinforced by a number of parallels linking Mag with Teddy. She too is "incontinent of faeces and water" (17), having reached an advanced stage of decrepitude — "deaf, blind, impotent, mad old woman" (19). She also reeks of the gangrene of old age, "odour of antiquity" (19). Since Molloy already has much in common with his mother, and will increasingly resemble her, by analogy he shares the fate of Teddy: "... we were like a couple of old cronies, sexless, unrelated, with the same memories, the same rancours, the same expectations" (17).

Thus Molloy's presence in the world and, by implication, ours as well, is the result of an arbitrary, biological process; we are whelped rather than born. Between birth and an uncertain death lies a humiliating dog's life during the course of which one becomes no better than Teddy, stinking, infirm, and discarded. It is small wonder, then, that Molloy rejects having been brought into the world by this old cur, responsible for having initiated the "whole sordid, malodorous, obscene Calvary-procession from womb to refuse-dump." [3]

The dog image is also employed to depict Molloy's relationship with Edith. Here the dog is used as a symbol of lust and lasciviousness. The human sexual act is reduced to animalistic physicality when Molloy and Edith make love like the random coupling of dogs in the street. Molloy

---

[3] Richard N. Coe, *Samuel Beckett* (New York: Grove Press, 1964), p. 57.

enters Edith from the rear: "It seemed all right to me, for I had seen dogs, and I was astonished when she confided that you could go about it differently" (57). At the height of his passion Molloy bites Edith: "And all I could see was her taught yellow nape which every now and then I set my teeth in, forgetting I had none, such is the power of instinct" (57). Such relationships may lead, of course, to the birth of yet another dog. Ultimately, Molloy prefers the more cerebral pleasures of masturbation.

Society too has its animalistic aspect, and this is accentuated during the course of Molloy's voyage. During Molloy's "golden moment" the arresting officer gently pushes his prisoner's bicycle "with the tips of his white-gloved fingers" (20-21). Those who watch them pass evince only tranquility. But society's veneer of humanity is easily effaced. After Molloy runs over Teddy his treatment is far different. Now the policeman's hand has become the menacing paw of an animal: "He brought down heavily on my handlebars his big red hairy paw" (33). The policeman is only an extension of the citizenry. The latter suggest a pack of dogs as they prepare to dispatch the prey they have run to ground: "... I made things worse by trying to run away. I was soon overtaken by a bloodthirsty mob of both sexes and all ages ... and they were preparing to tear me apart when the lady intervened" (32). The image of society as a hunting pack reappears, this time explicitly, in Molloy's depiction of the "exterminators": "They wake up, hale and hearty, their tongues hanging out for order, beauty and justice, baying for their due" (67).[4]

In the second half of the novel Beckett further establishes the man-dog relationship. Moran is compared to a

---

[4] In the original the "mob" that pursues Molloy after he runs over Teddy is described as a "meute" (47), which figuratively signifies a group of people banded against an individual but in the context of the incident keeps its literal meaning, a "pack of hunting dogs." This dog image has been reinserted here, in the description of the exterminators. The French reads: "Les gens se réveillent, frais et dispos, assoiffés d'ordre, de beauté et de justice, exigeant la contre-partie" (101).

neighbor's dog, Zulu, by means of a mirror-like parallelism
as he and the dog contemplate each other through a fence.
Moran's attention to Zulu's genitalia reflects the same association between human sexuality and the dog's indiscrim-
inate sexuality present in Molloy's relations with Edith:
"Crouching down I would stroke his ears, through the
railings, and utter wheedling words. He did not realize he
disgusted me. He reared up on his hind legs and pressed
his chest against the bars. Then I could see his little black
penis ending in a thin wisp of wetted hair. He felt insecure,
his hams trembled, his little paws fumbled for purchase,
one after the other. I too wobbled, squatting on my heels.
With my free hand I held on to the railings. Perhaps I
disgusted him too" (105). Moran's disgust and obvious fascination with what he sees reflects his own attitude toward
sex. He satisfies his own needs by means of masturbation
but regrets having a son; and he attempts to inculcate in
the boy "that most fruitful of dispositions, horror of the
body and its functions" (118).

Although Moran has been ordered to take his son with
him, he also needs the boy because he is somewhat afraid
of facing his mission alone. He thinks of putting his son
on a leash, as if he were a dog: "I toyed briefly with the
idea of attaching him to me by means of a long rope ..."
(129). And continuing to muse upon this possibility, Moran
goes even further: "... imagining myself in a world less ill
contrived and wondering how, having nothing more than
a simple chain, without collar or band or gyves or fetters
of any kind, I could chain my son to me in such a way
as to prevent him from ever shaking me off again" (129).
Moran's son's constipation on the day of departure and Moran's desire to exploit his son in order to compensate for
his own insecurity link the Moran *père*-Moran *fils* relationship to that of A and his pomeranian.

Ironically, when Moran meets the shepherd, he thinks
of abandoning his quest and exchanging its uncertainties
for a comfortable life with the shepherd as a sort of sheep
dog: "I longed to say, Take me with you, I will serve you
faithfully, just for a place to lie and a little food" (159).

Moran's reverie is terminated by an element of doubt: "But the dog stops at the threshold [of the shepherd's cottage], not knowing whether he may go in or whether he must stay out, all night" (160). This wistful vision of the dog's life differs radically from the one Molloy is living out. Plainly, there is no escape for Moran from the pain and mystery of his quest, nor from the destiny that will transform him into an old dog like Molloy.

Despite the changes that Moran is undergoing and will inexorably continue to undergo, he is linked to Lousse and to A by the image of the dog. These are the individuals who victimize, or attempt to victimize, the weak, treating them as dogs in a vain attempt to evade or deny their own loneliness or abandonment. The relationship of A and C to the dog reinforces their role as projections of Moran and Molloy. A exploits the dog, whereas C resembles the creature he exploits. Their respective designations and the opposition between the bourgeois and the wanderer further identify them with Abel and Cain.[5] Just as the latter represent two aspects of humanity, so too in *Molloy* the characters' associations with the dog divide them into two groups. Ultimately of course they are one, all Cains, all old dogs, each wearing the chain and collar he inherits at birth.[6]

The respective relationships of Molloy and Moran with the sheep and lambs they meet sheds additional light on their contrasting roles. Molloy expresses an identification with the members of the flock when the shepherd's dog stares at him: "Did he take me for a black sheep entangled in the brambles and was he waiting for an order from his master to drag me out? I don't think so. I don't smell like

---

[5] The Abel-Cain relationship is less obvious in the French, where the two figures are designated as A and B. Absent from the translation, however, is Molloy's reference to them as "mes deux larrons" (61). The two thieves crucified with Christ, one damned and one saved, represent two aspects of humanity and can be considered as analogues of Abel and Cain.

[6] See Ross Chambers, "The Artist as Performing Dog, *Comparative Literature*, 23 (Fall 1971), 312-324.

a sheep. I wish I smelt like a sheep, or a buck-goat" (28). Molloy's desire to be one of the sheep is a death wish, a wish to abandon his quest and accompany the flock to the slaughterhouse. There, he would meet a certain end, however horrible, stretched out on the butcher's block. But Molloy, of course, cannot be one and his existence will continue to be a Calvary "with no limit to its stations and no hope of crucifixion" (78). Molloy is Christ, Lamb of God, without the Passion.

The sheep "entangled in the brambles" recalls the story of Abraham and Isaac. In the case of Molloy, Beckett is not concerned with the human characters in the Biblical episode but with the animal victim sacrificed in Isaac's place. The members of the shepherd's flock are no less innocent than the ram Abraham slaughtered; they will be slain through the agency of a "cosmic cruelty"[7] no more comprehensible than the justice demanded by the God of the Old Testament.

The allusion to Abraham and Isaac links the two shepherd episodes and further elucidates the relationship of Moran to his son. Moran, no less obedient than Abraham, submits to Youdi's request that he take his son with him on his journey: "I was not going to expose myself to thunderbolts which might be fatal, simply because my son had the gripes. If he fell seriously ill on the way, it would be another matter. It was not for nothing I had studied the Old Testament" (183). Symbolically, Moran *fils* is sacrificed, for, as a consequence of his father's quest, he is torn unwillingly from childhood and initiated into harsh reality.

Moran's role as Abraham is affirmed as well by the reaction of the sheep to him. Whereas Molloy took the part of the victim, Moran emerges as the executioner: "Now I was in the midst of the sheep, they made a circle around me, their eyes converged on me. Perhaps I was the butcher come to make his choice" (159). Yet if Moran cannot be

---

[7] Ruby Cohn, *Samuel Beckett: The Comic Gamut* (New Brunswick, New Jersey: Rutgers University Press, 1962), p. 152.

where Molloy is not, then one day he too will long to be one of the sheep.

The two meetings with the shepherd, especially Molloy's, indicate the importance the slaughterhouse assumes in the novel. Molloy describes in detail the terrible death of the lambs: "... fallen, their skulls shattered, their thin legs crumpling, first to their knees, then over on their fleecy sides, under the pole-axe ..." (29).[8] Molloy's vision of the island he inhabits is that of a land in which slaughterhouses abound. If the hostility of his fellow men were not enough to reveal to him the precarious nature of existence, then the ubiquity of the shambles would remind him — and us — that the reward of innocence is the butcher's knife: "Where are you taking them, to the field or to the shambles? I must have completely lost my sense of direction, as if direction had anything to do with the matter. For even if he was going towards the town, what prevented him from skirting it, or from leaving it again by another gate, on his way to new pastures, and if he was going away from it that meant nothing either, for slaughter-houses are not confined to towns, no, they are everywhere, the country is full of them, every butcher has his slaughter-house and the right to slaughter, according to his lights" (28-29).

Molloy's sensitivity to the presence of the abattoir is no doubt a product of long familiarity. His birth was heralded by the cries of the animals being led to their deaths, for his mother's room is located in the same district as the slaughterhouses: "... from my mother's room, through the closed windows I had heard, stilling her chatter, the

---

[8] The English translation adds a qualification absent from the French, "though that is not the way they slaughter sheep, but with a knife, so that they bled to death" (29). Although his description of the death of the sheep and lambs is no less effective, Beckett confuses their slaughter with that of cattle. The latter are indeed stunned to death, either with a hammer or, in the modern abattoir, with a pneumatic gun. Sheep and lambs, on the other hand, are stretched out on the butcher's table preparatory to having their throats slit. The addition to the English text corrects the mistake in the original and, more importantly perhaps, permits Beckett to augment the horror of the scene he is depicting.

bellowing of the cattle, that violent raucous tremulous bellowing . . ." (22).

Like Mag, Moran also lives near a slaughterhouse. But
he, as well as his son, is indifferent to its presence. This
attitude, reinforced by the image of Moran as the butcher
and contrasted with Molloy's concern, suggests once again
that only by becoming a victim can Moran acquire both
an insight into the human condition and an appreciation
of the suffering endured by those who mutely share man's
misery.

During Molloy's stay at Lousse's house, a rapport is
established between him and Lousse's parrot: "I understood him better than his mistress. . . . I understood him
better than I understood her" (37). Their "understanding"
is based upon more than a fondness for the scatological
or the imprisonment they share. More importantly, they
speak the same language.

A man's speech should, for obvious reasons, be superior
to that of a parrot. But Molloy finds that the words he
hears spoken by others make as little sense to him as the
words he himself utters. Emptied of meaning, they become
mere sounds and are mimicked — as a parrot simply imitates the sounds of the words he hears:

> Yes, the words I heard, and heard distinctly, having
> quite a sensitive ear, were heard a first time, then
> a second, and often even a third, as pure sounds,
> free of all meaning, and this is probably one of the
> reasons why conversation was unspeakably painful
> to me. And the words I uttered myself, and which
> must always have gone with an effort of the intel-
> ligence, were often to me as the buzzing of an in-
> sect. And this is perhaps one of the reasons I was
> so untalkative, I mean this trouble I had in under-
> standing not only what others said to me but also
> what I said to them. It is true that in the end, by
> dint of patience, we made ourselves understood, but
> understood with regard to what, I ask of you, and
> to what purpose? (50)

The problem lies, of course, with the nature of language
itself. The words we inherit from others, which we imitate,

inadequately communicate our own reality. And the deeper we penetrate into that reality, the more insufficient language becomes. The use of language thus turns out to be a parrot-like repetition, like the squawking of mindless obscenities: "You invent nothing, you think you are inventing, you think you are inventing, you think you are escaping, and all you do is stammer out your lesson, the remnants of a pensum one day got by heart and long forgotten, life without tears, as it is wept. To hell with it anyway" (32).

The Molloy-parrot association is echoed in the Moran-Moran *fils* couple. When Moran gives his son instructions concerning the purchase of a bicycle, he discovers that his words make no sense to the boy. His misplaced faith in language and in the efficacy of verbal communication cause him to misinterpret his son's bewilderment as a sign of stupidity or a gesture of defiance: "He did not understand.... He came back towards me. I waved him away, crying, Go on! Go on! He stopped and stared at me, his head on one side like a parrot, utterly bewildered apparently.... I reached up above my head, broke off a live bough and hurled it violently in his direction" (144).

Several animals appear in Molloy's narration that are not present in Moran's. One of these is the ass. By juxtaposing Molloy cycling along the tow path and an ass on the opposite bank hauling a barge, Beckett suggests an analogy between these two beasts of burden. In the symbolism derived from the New Testament, the ass — the animal Christ rode when he entered Jerusalem — "bears the weight of the unintelligible world, as Christian bore a crushing burden till he reached the foot of the cross."[9] The ass in *Molloy*, however, is a surrogate for Christ. He hauls the materials of which the cross is made, a cargo of nails and timber, and he is lashed by the "angry cries and dull blows" (26) of the bargeman. Molloy, the human Christ-figure of the episode, must bear the burden of a decaying

---

[9] See Jack Lindsay's "Introduction" to his translation of Apuleius' *The Golden Ass* (Bloomington, Indiana: Midland Books, 1962), p. 13.

body in an equally brutal and incomprehensible world, one without hope of crucifixion. He, a man, envies the strength and patience of the ass: "My eyes caught on a donkey's eyes, they fell to his little feet, their brave fastidious tread" (26).

Lousse's parrot is not the only bird that appears in Molloy's narration. The time of Molloy's departure coincides with the mating season of the corncrakes. His reaction to the sounds of reproduction that fill the countryside is consonant with his execration of his own birth and underlines the significance of his voyage as both an expiation for having been born and a quest for rebirth: ". . . it would ill become me not to mention the awful cries of the corncrakes that run in the corn, in the meadows, all the short summer night long, dinning their rattles" (16). [10]

Having placed the commencement of Molloy's journey under the sign of the corncrake, Beckett places its conclusion under the sign of the lark: "I lapsed down to the bottom of the ditch. It must have been spring, a morning in spring. I thought I heard birds, skylarks perhaps" (91). The song of the lark with its traditional evocation of the joys of fertility and revival puts, as did the rattle of the corncrakes, the sense of Molloy's journey into sharper focus. The seeming contradiction between Molloy's collapse and all that the lark's song connotes only emphasizes the necessity of Molloy's dying to the world in order to be reborn.

Several animals are unique to Moran's part of the novel. One of them is an ailing gray hen. The "justice" of the henhouse does not surprise us for the law of nature decrees that the weak member of the species must perish. We may

---

[10] Dieter Wellershof, noting how Beckett "mixes" his images, interprets the corncrakes as quail (the close resemblance between the two species has led to their mingling in bird legends) and, consequently, as a symbol of birth: "Zeus transformed himself and Lete into quail and begat Artemis with her, who was considered the goddess of birth and to whom the quail was dedicated as her sacred bird." "Failure of An Attempt at De-Mythologization," in *Samuel Beckett: A Collection of Critical Essays,* ed. Martin Esslin (Englewood Cliffs, New Jersey: Spectrum Books, 1965), p. 96.

ask ourselves, however, if human justice, as shown in *Molloy*, is truly more enlightened. Molloy's situation with respect to the mob that pursues him after he has run over Teddy or to the packs of exterminators that force him to hide by day, parallels that of the grey hen: "My grey hen was there, not on the perch with the others, but on the ground, in a corner, in the dust, at the mercy of the rats. The cock no longer sought her out to tread her angrily. The day was at hand, if she did not take a turn for the better, when the other hens would join forces and tear her to bits with their beaks and claws" (128). Father Ambrose's passing remark that the chicken sitting in the dust reminded him of Job also recalls Molloy's plight. There is no rational explanation for the suffering Molloy undergoes, but, unlike Job, there is no God in whom he can put his faith and hence be rescued from his dung heap. The first visitor to Moran's camp is, for similar reasons, compared to a chicken: ". . . he made a curious movement, like a hen that puffs up its feathers and slowly dwindles till it is smaller than before" (146). Lastly, one can compare Moran himself with the gray hen. Having once thought of himself as strong and secure, he is the victim of several hostile encounters as he drags himself, debilitated and in rags, home. Only his guile saves him from the belligerence and aggressiveness of his fellow men.

Moran also raises bees, not so much for their honey as for the fascination their dance — the intricate combinations of movements and sounds they make — provides him. Given the number of determinates that enter into the dance and their variability, it becomes a subject that is inexhaustible, and Moran avows: "Here is something I can study all my life and never understand" (169):

> The most striking feature of the dance was its very complicated figures, traced in flight, and I had classified a great number of these with their probable meanings. But there was also the question of the hum, so various in tone in the vicinity of the hive that this could hardly be an effect of chance. I first concluded that each figure was reinforced by means

of a hum peculiar to it. But I was forced to abandon this agreeable hypothesis. For I saw the same figure (at least what I called the same figure) accompanied by very different hums. So that I said, The purpose of the hum is not to emphasize the dance, but on the contrary to vary it. And the same figure exactly differs in meaning according to the hum that goes with it. And I had collected and classified a great number of observations on this subject, with gratifying results. But there was also to be considered not only the figure and the hum, but also the height at which the figure was executed. (168-169)

The dance of Moran's bees can be interpreted as a representation of reality, such as Beckett conceives it. Under scrutiny it reveals itself to be a meaningless set of particulars; and the more one analyzes it, the more particulars and combinations of particulars one finds. They lack meaning because they lack a unifying principle or pattern. As long as the data remains incomplete — as Moran constantly finds new elements that enter into the dance — one can only draw hypotheses or establish statistical probabilities.

However, as we might suspect, there is always the strong possibility that there is no meaning whatsoever amid this whirl of phenomena, that there is simply nothing at their center. Confronted with a mystery such as that of the bees' dance, human beings, with their natural desire to transform the inexplicable into the explicable, the illogical into the logical, habitually falsify the nature of things by giving them a coherence, a sense they do not inherently possess. One means of achieving this is, of course, to impose upon a phenomenon the logic of language. Moran, on the other hand, claims to study the bees without recourse to his anthropomorphic prejudice. Thus he compares the bees' dance to God, the epitome of that which is incomprehensible and ineffable: "And I would never do my bees the wrong I had done my God, to whom I had been taught to ascribe my angers, fears, desires, and even my body" (169).

When Moran returns home he discovers the bees have died during his absence. Now the dance of the bees can no longer be a subject of idle speculation. Moran himself

has been initiated into the sort of world for which the bees'
dance served as a metaphor. Both the coherence he himself
once so speciously imposed upon his life and the identity
he so artfully contrived crumble away like the handful of
dead bees Moran pulls from the hive. A remark by Molloy
sums up Moran's future as it echos the image of the bees'
dance: "Yes, it's all easy when you know why, a mere
matter of magic. Yes, the whole thing is to know what saint
to implore, any fool can implore him. For the particulars,
if you are interested in particulars, there is no need to
despair, you may scrabble on the right door, in the right
way, in the end. It's for the whole there seems to be no
spell. Perhaps there is no whole, before you're dead" (27).

Bees are not the only insects that figure in Moran's narration. He is also fascinated by certain flies. Moran recalls
an incident with a fly while he is describing the period he
spent torpid and feeble in his camp on the outskirts of
Bally. The juxtaposition of the two descriptions creates an
affective link between the fragility of the insect and that
of the man: "And I note here the little beat my heart once
missed, in my home, when a fly, flying low above my ash-
tray, raised a little ash, with the breath of its wings. And
I grew gradually weaker and weaker and more and more
content" (162).

This comparison between Moran and a fly is extended
by Moran's evocation of a particular species of fly. Moran's
attention is drawn to them because he sees in the life cycle
of these strange insects an ideal state, one close to the
sort of oblivion into which he had fallen while waiting in
his camp. He idly dreams of a warm, somnolent existence,
free of pain, suffering, quests, and procreation, an existence terminated by an easy death: "But to return to the
flies, I like to think of those that hatch out at the beginning of winter, within doors, and die shortly after. You see
them crawling and fluttering in the warm corners, puny,
sluggish, torpid, mute. That is you see an odd one now and
then. They must die very young, without having been able
to lay. You sweep them away, you push them into the

dustpan with the brush, without knowing. That is a strange race of flies" (166).

As was the case in Molloy's narration, certain birds appear at the beginning and at the end of Moran's part of the novel. Moran hears the hoot of the eagle-owl as he begins his report. The owl, the traditional herald of gloom and disaster, foreshadows with its cry the catastrophe that Moran is about to relate: "What a terrible battle-cry. Once I listened to it unmoved" (92). When Moran returns home his chickens, the domestic birds associated with his former mode of existence, are dead. Moran's attention turns toward the wild birds that frequent his garden, with which he establishes a new relationship. Moran himself is about to become a sort of wild bird, a solitary, wandering creature, as he prepares to resume his quest. He will therefore abandon his old attachments, including, if he can, his old language in order to pursue his quarry: "My birds had not been killed. They were wild birds. And yet quite trusting. I recognized them and they seemed to recognize me. But one never knows. Some were missing and some were new. I tried to understand their language better. Without recourse to mine" (175).

III

Like the protagonists of *Molloy*, Malone depreciates sexual relations by associating them with the coupling of dogs. Looking at a couple framed in a window across the street, he assumes: "They have loved each other standing, like dogs. Soon they will be able to part. Or perhaps they are just having a breather, before they tackle the titbit" (238). Having been born into the dog's life, Malone, old and infirm like Teddy, finds an analogy for his present situation in the pathetic plight of a hunting dog no longer of any use to its master: "To old dogs the hour comes when, whistled by their master setting forth with his stick at dawn, they cannot spring after him. Then they stay in their kennel, or in their basket, though they are not chained, and listen to the steps dying away. The man too is sad. But soon the pure air and the sun console him, he thinks no more about his old companion, until evening. The lights in his house bid him welcome home and a feeble barking makes him say, It is time I had him destroyed" (191-192). There is no one however to put Malone to sleep, to afford him a simple death. Instead, he must perform the task himself, putting himself to sleep, as it were, with his "homuncules."

Malone recalls that a Jewish acquaintance of his, named Jackson, used to call him the "merino" because, he tells us, of the "French expression" (218).[11] Beckett makes an elaborate play here on the word "merino," which, literally, refers to a variety of sheep. The French expression to which he alludes is *laisser pisser les mérinos*. Usually, it is employed figuratively and means "to wait patiently"; as such it may foreshadow Malone's future circumstances. There is no doubt, however, about Jackson's literal use of the expression, "let the merinos piss," for when Malone and Jackson meet for the first time, the former urinates in his pants.

"Merino," as Malone himself notes, is derived from a Spanish word meaning "wandering herd." Thus Malone, thinking no doubt of the wandering Israelites — the flock of Moses the shepherd — comments that the word is "better adapted" (218) to Jackson than to himself. But Jackson did not misname Malone. Malone himself has been a wanderer, at first physically and later verbally. And just as Molloy compared himself to the Jews in the desert when he spoke of his being lost in an "Egypt without bounds," so too Malone must remain in exile until he can be born into the Promised Land of the self.

In *Malone Dies*, the beast of burden takes the form of a horse. He hauls a cab this time but under the ever-present

---

[11] "Because of the French expression" augments the original "à cause du dicton" (81). Having alerted his reader (which Beckett felt compelled to do in French as well), Beckett keeps in the translation an elaborate play on words that has no equivalent in English and cannot be understood without a knowledge of French.

lash of the driver. His cargo is, however, human, and it is through a description of the sort of people who ride in the taxi that the image of the horse is defined. They are people who have just left their offices at the end of the work day and who, suddenly finding themselves severed from the ties of routine and all alone, fear and seek the warmth of human company. Thus both horse and men have their respective burdens. Whereas the former cannot evade his, the latter attempt to evade theirs. The human burden is not only a decaying body — a condition which the man shares with the horse — but also the crushing solitude that is an inescapable part of the human condition. And until their defective body-machines stop functioning, they lose themselves in a purposeless coming and going, no different from a dumb animal: "And so they hasten, the horse, the driver and the passenger, towards the appointed place, by the shortest route or deviously, through the press of other misplaced persons. And each one has his reasons, while wondering from time to time what they are worth, and if they are the true ones, for going where he is going rather than somewhere else, and the horse hardly less darkly than the men" (231).

The cab-horse's fate is certain. When he is no longer capable of doing his job, he will be dispatched to the shambles. In *Malone Dies*, however, the theme of cruel and arbitrary death is conveyed not by the ubiquitous abattoir but through the character of Big Lambert, the amateur butcher who takes such a delight in his work: "From these expeditions he reached home late in the night, drunk and exhausted by the long road and the emotions of the day. And for days afterwards he would speak of nothing but the pig he had just dispatched..." (200). [12]

---

[12] Another passage describing the love Big Lambert (Gros Louis in French) lavishes on his "hobby" as well as his pride in the skill he has developed at it has been deleted from the translation: "Car il aimait ce travail et était fier de savoir si bien le faire, en artiste, selon le secret que son père lui avait transmis et dont il se considérait le dernier dépositaire" (46).

Big Lambert's most active period occurs during Christmas time. Beckett employs this "coincidence" to emphasize Big Lambert's cruelty — and, indirectly, that of the people who need his services so that they may enjoy a Christmas ham — by calling our attention to the event that Christmas celebrates. And he invites us to recall the traditional image of the Child in the manger being watched over by two animals — an ass and an ox. The animals Big Lambert slaughters are no less innocent than those that attended Jesus' birth or the Infant Jesus himself: "His great days then fell in December and January, and from February onwards he waited impatiently for the return of that season, the principal event of which is unquestionably the Saviour's birth, in a stable, while wondering if he would be spared till then" (200).

Having associated Big Lambert's activities with the birth of Christ, Beckett associates them as well with Christ's death. In choosing between which one of two kids he will slaughter, Big Lambert evokes one of Beckett's familiar motifs, that of the two thieves crucified with Christ — one of whom was saved and one of whom was damned according to the Gospel of Saint Luke. When Big Lambert makes his choice, he arrogates to himself the power of God, a cruel and arbitrary God, according to Beckett — one who loves some of us some of the time and whose inscrutable justice affords us at best a fifty-fifty chance of being saved: "After a silence Lambert declared, I'll kill Whitey tomorrow. . . . But neither his wife nor his son could approve him, the former because she would have preferred him to kill Blackey, the latter because he held that to kill the kids at such an early stage of their development, either of them, it was all the same to him, would be premature. But Big Lambert told them to hold their tongues and went to the corner to fetch the case containing the knives . . ." (215).

Curiously, however, it is Malone who appears to share Big Lambert's penchant for slaughter. Malone does his killing verbally, by means of detailed, very matter-of-fact descriptions of the ways in which various species of animals are killed:

There are rabbits that die before they are killed, from sheer fright. They have time to do so while being taken out of the hutch, often by the ears, and disposed in the most convenient position to receive the blow, whether on the back of the neck or on some other part. For you have just seen the rabbit alive and well behind the wire meshing, nibbling at its leaves. And you congratulate yourself on having succeeded with the first blow, and not caused unnecessary suffering, whereas in reality you have taken all that trouble for nothing. This occurs most frequently at night, fright being greater in the night. Hens on the other hand are more stubborn livers and some have been observed, with the head already off, to cut a few last capers before collapsing. Pigeons too are less impressionable and sometimes even struggle before choking to death. (214-215).

The tone of Malone's description, with its detachment and objectivity, coupled with his sensitive evocation of the hunting dog and the cab-horse would seem to suggest that he is using irony here to condemn the sort of existence in which such slaughtering takes place as well as the indifference with which it is viewed. Then too he may also be expressing an identification with the animal victims, a longing for a definitive end. Sapo evinces these very sentiments upon watching, at the Lambert farm, the burial of an old mule: "A great calm stole over him. Great calm is an exaggeration. He felt better. The end of life is always vivifying" (212).

Sapo is also fascinated by the flight of a hawk. He, like the hawk, is a solitary creature but, unlike the bird of prey he admires, he lacks the qualities that would permit him to transcend his isolation and abandonment. Moreover, Sapo's furtive movements and his manner of walking as if he were wading through a bog are the very antithesis of the hawk's flight: "...he loved the flight of the hawk and could distinguish it from all others. He would stand rapt, gazing at the long pernings, the quivering poise, the wings lifted for the plummet drop, the wild reascent, fascinated by such extremes of need, of pride, of patience and solitude" (191).[13]

Although Sapo wishes to resemble a hawk, he more closely resembles a chicken — notably a particular grey hen that he encounters when he withdraws into the darkness of the Lambert kitchen. The contrast between the two birds accentuates Sapo's retiring nature and, ultimately, his rejection of reality. Sapo and the hen have several traits in common. The grey hen seems to exist apart from the other members of the flock, just as Sapo has a limited relationship with his fellow men. And, like Sapo, the grey hen hesitates to abandon the outside world of light and noise and confusion. But she too yields to the fascination that the darkness profers: "... this big, anxious, ashen bird, poised irresolute on the bright threshold, then clucking and clawing behind the range and fidgeting her atrophied wings, soon to be sent flying with a broom and angry cries and soon to return, cautiously, with little hesitant steps, stopping often to listen, opening and shutting her little bright black eyes" (204).

Birds evolved from reptiles just as man himself sprang from creatures that crawled upon the ground. The same dehumanization that resulted from Molloy's voyage and forced Molloy to finally abandon the upright position affects Macmann as well. Beckett employs the bird-reptile relationship to characterize this process. Speculation upon the reasons for his suffering under the rain lies beyond Macmann's capabilities: "But these are flights for which Macmann was not yet fledged, and indeed he was rather of the earth earthy and ill-fitted for pure reason.... And to tell the truth he was by temperament more reptile

---

[13] Sapo's admiration of the hawk recalls similar sentiments on the part of Stendhal's Julien Sorel: "From time to time a hawk from the great cliffs above his head caught his eye, soaring in vast silent circles. Julien's eye followed the bird of prey mechanically. Its calm and powerful motion impressed him, he envied that strength, he envied that isolation." *The Red and The Black*, trans. Joan Charles (Philadelphia and Toronto: John C. Winston Co., 1949), p. 24.

than bird and could suffer extensive mutilation and survive ..." (243).

Beckett is playing here on the words "flight" and "fledged." Metaphorically, they refer to the absence of reasoning power that would permit Macmann to find an explanation for his situation — if indeed there were one. At the same time, Beckett preserves their original meaning by comparing Macmann to an actual bird. Literalism and metaphor combine to reinforce the depiction of Macmann as just the opposite of a bird, as a lowly creature glued to the earth by an existence whose hostility is beyond his — and our — comprehension.

Jackson, like Lousse, owned a parrot: "He used to try and teach it to say, Nihil in intellectu, etc. These first three words the bird managed well enough, but the celebrated restriction was too much for it, all you heard was a series of squawks. This annoyed Jackson, who kept nagging at it to begin over again. Then Polly flew into a rage and retreated to a corner of its cage" (218). The "restriction" the parrot is unable to utter is the second part of the Scholastic axiom that reads in full, *Nihil in intellectu quod non prius in sensu* — our thoughts and knowledge are derived from the experience of our senses.

The parrot's words summarize Malone's own situation. Beckett rejects of course the primacy of sense data, as Descartes did when he made self-consciousness the locus of his epistemology. [14] As we see in the case of the voyager-turned-author, the degeneration of the body's sensory apparatus is compensated for by an increase in mental activity

---

[14] Descartes writes in his *Discourse on Method*: "What makes many people feel that it is difficult to know of the existence of God, or even of the nature of their own souls, is that they never withdraw their minds from their senses and consider things higher than corporeal objects.... This is also manifest in the fact that even philosophers hold it as a maxim in the schools that there is nothing in the understanding which was not first in the senses, a location where it is clearly evident that the ideas of God and of the soul have never been." *Discourse on Method and Meditations*, trans. Laurence Lafleur (New York: The Library of Liberal Arts, 1960), p. 28.

— his voyage becomes verbal. Now Malone's problem is precisely to have nothing in his mind, to empty the mental microcosm so that he can be reborn. And we see this phenomenon ocurring at the end of the novel when noises of evacuation accompany his birth in death. But until that moment of liberation comes, Malone's situation resembles the parrot's. He is a garrulous old man imprisoned in a room repeating the words of an acquired language. Malone's reaction to the parrot's cage reveals his awareness of the resemblance between man and bird: "It was a very fine cage, with every convenience, perches, swings, trays, troughs, stairs and cuttlebones. It was even overcrowded, personally I would have felt cramped" (218).

IV

Anticipating his return to the blockhouse, Mahood compares himself to a dog, using an image that recalls the constipated pomeranian that A snatched up in his arms. This figure explicitly qualifies Mahood's existence as a dog's life and, through the analogies we have already establised, puts him on the side of the animal victims: "When I penetrate into that house, if I ever do, it will be to go on turning, faster and faster, more and more convulsive, like a constipated dog, or one suffering from worms ..." (321). Worm, the Unnamable's other "vice-exister," is also treated like a dog — in his case by the "delegates" who attempt, with their words, to make him one of them. If permitted to develop, Worm is destined to become just another Mahood. Thus Worm is "like a dog that always gets the same filth flung to it, the same orders, the same threats, the same cajoleries" (359).

Finally, the image of the dog's life characterizes the futile and endless interplay between the Unnamable, Mahood, and Worm — or, theoretically, any number of "vice-existers" created through the quest for self. No sooner does one "dog" die off then another takes its place, to participate in the same destiny. Thus the dog's song, the same one Vladimir sings in *Waiting for Godot*, with its figure of the dog and its repetitive structure serves as a metaphor for the solipsism in which the Unnamable is enmeshed: A dog crawled into the kitchen and stole a crust of bread, then cook up with I've forgotten what and walloped him till he was dead, second verse, Then all the dogs came crawling and dug the dog a tomb and wrote upon the tombstone for dogs and bitches to come, third verse, as the first, fourth, as the second, fifth, as the third, give us time, and we'll be a multitude ..." (379).

The Unnamable, like Molloy, evokes the image of the lamb being led to the slaughter. But in this instance the cruelty of the macrocosm has been replaced by that of the microcosm, and the "delegates" have supplanted the butchers. The Unnamable refuses to fall victim to the shambles, to succomb to language and join the fictions he has rejected: "One of us at last! Green with anguish! A real little terrestrial! Choking in the chlorophyll! Hugging the slaughter-house walls! Paltry priests of the irrepressible ephemeral, how they must hate me. Come my lambkin, join in our gambols, it's soon over, you'll see, just time to frolic with a lambkinette, that's jam" (316).

In addition to his being compared to a dog, Mahood is also compared to a horse. The compulsion to move combined with his deteriorating physical condition has transformed him into a dumb beast of burden. Unlike the horse described in *Malone Dies*, Mahood cannot even conceive of a respite from the coming and going that is his life: "This obligation, and the quasi-impossibility of fulfilling it, engrossed me in a purely mechanical way, excluding notably the free play of the intelligence and sensibility, so that my situation rather resembled that of an old broken-down cart or bat-horse unable to receive the least information either from its instinct or from its observation as to whether it is moving towards the stable or away from it ..." (320).

This same image of the horse and the stable reappears, with reference this time to the dilemma of the Unnamable. His burden is that of the words he bears in his quest for silence. And it is this perpetual quest that prevents him

from returning to his particular stable — the void — a
stable which, as the essential self, he has never left: "I'm
off, you wouldn't think so, perhaps it's my last gallop, I
smell the stable, I always smelt the stable, it's I smell of
the stable, there's no stable but me, for me" (400-401).

The jar in which Mahood terminates his voyage is located in the rue Brancion, in the district of the shambles. [15]
The empty eyes of a horse's bust, the insignia in France of
a horse-butcher's shop, stare down to remind him that for
some voyagers the journey of life has come to a definitive
end: "If I turn, I shall not say my head, but my eyes, free
to roll as they list, I can see the statue of the apostle of
horse's meat, a bust. His pupilless eyes of stone are fixed
upon me. That makes four, with those of my creator, om-
nipresent, do not imagine I flatter myself I am privileged"
(327). Mahood's reference to his "creator's" eyes reveals
both the bond of sympathy that exists between him and
the horse-victim and a condemnation of the malevolent
deity that could be held responsible for their fate. That
same fate is extended to Worm, who is born with "a wild
equine eye" (357).

Bombarded by the cries of animals being led to the
slaughterhouses, Mahood expresses a familiar death wish,
to be dispatched with the other victims: "If only the earth
would quake! The shambles swallow me up" (341). But the

---

[15] John Fletcher notes that the location of Mahood's jar has a
basis in reality: "... there was formerly an eating house called the
'Ali-Baba' with, appropriately enough, a 'thief' outside it, fixed in a
jar, supporting the menu. Beckett places it in the novel ... in the
rue Brancion, facing the bust of the propagator of horse-meat,
Emile Decroix; this bust is set over the eastern entrance of the
Vaugirard abattoirs in the fifteenth *arrondissement*. The real Ali-
Baba stood, however, in the rue de Dantzig, on the western side
of the abattoirs, near a dilapidated round wooden building inhabited
by artists (*La Ruche*) which may well have suggested the ... rotunda
in which Mahood's family live.... Beckett would have known it
since he lived at one time in the rue des Favorites, not far away."
The Novels of Samuel Beckett (London: Chatto and Windus, 1964),
pp. 184-185. See also Rayner Heppenstall, *The Fourfold Tradition:
Notes on the French and English literatures with some ethnological
and historical asides* (London: Barrie and Rockliff, 1961), p. 261.

site of Mahood's jar permits Beckett to enlarge the scope of the image of the abattoir beyond its application to the existence of his protagonist. He also focuses on those average citizens who, each in his own way, are accomplices to the slaughter of the innocent. There are those whose tender sensibilities are their excuse for not confronting the horror of the abattoir: "... that category of hypersensitive persons for whom the least thing is an occasion for scandal and indignation. ... such people avoiding the neighborhood for fear of being overcome at the sight of the cattle, fat and fresh from their pastures, trooping towards the humane killer" (327). On the other hand, some people delight in the sight and sounds of this perfectly inhumane killing: "... the idlers come to hear the cattle's bellows of pain and who, time obviously heavy on their hands, pace up and down waiting for the slaughter to begin" (341). Lastly, there are the indifferent. They lack the sensitive ears of the Unnamable who hears in the mingling of the anguished cries of the animals with the sounds of the diners eating the products of the abattoir a horrible symphony: "I left it yesterday, Mahood's world, the street, the chop-house, the slaughter, the statue and, through the railings, the sky like a slate-pencil, I shall never again hear the lowing of the cattle, nor the clinking of the forks and glasses, nor the angry voices of the butchers, nor the litany of the dishes and the prices" (345).

On two occasions the Unnamable is compared to an owl. By means of the first of these images he portrays his confinement in his cage of words, in which, like an owl in a zoo, he is immobile and silent: "No, I have always been sitting here, at this selfsame spot ... like a great horned owl in an aviary" (293). The second image complements and extends the first. Instead of simply staring unblinkingly at his castoffs cercling around him or at the lights of his "delegates," he also closes his eyes in order to see scenes from his former life in the light. As we have already noted, the Unnamable's seeing is a result of his estrangement in language. Appropriately, he depicts this return to the world of men with a reference to an earlier incarnation, Murphy, who envied "the four caged owls in Battersea Park whose joys and sorrows did not begin until dusk" (106): "... like the owl cooped in Battersea Park, ah misery, will I never stop wanting a life for myself?" (393). In order to extinguish the lights and in order to cease being a spectator, the Unnamable must find the language of self that will permit him, like the owls mentioned in *Murphy*, to come alive in his element — in the darkness of the void.

As a prisoner of language, the Unnamable is a parrot. His is the same "pensum" that Molloy and Malone found themselves reiterating: "Yes, I have a pensum to discharge, before I can be free, free to dribble, free to speak no more, listen no more, and I've forgotten what it is. There at last is a fair picture of my situation. I was given a pensum at birth perhaps as a punishment for having been born perhaps, or for no particular reason, because they dislike me ..." (310). His existence having been usurped by the fictions born through his futile efforts to "discharge" this "pensum," he has become a mouthpiece for his "delegates": "It is they who dictate this torrent of balls, they who stuffed me full of these groans that choke me. And out it all pours unchanged. I have only to belch to be sure of hearing them, the same old sour teachings I can't change a title of. A parrot, that's what they're up against, a parrot" (335). [16]

The Unnamable's futile revolt against language is expressed as well by the image of the rat applied to the "delegates." In one instance the rat replaces the vulture in Greek mythology sent by Zeus to gnaw away at the liver of Prometheus. Unlike the latter, whose liver, consumed during the daytime, grew back at night so that his torture could be renewed, the Unnamable is granted no respite. The words of the "delegates" gnaw at him endlessly; his torture is a ceaseless fragmentation through fiction. A second image, that of a child in its cradle eaten by rats, serves to

---

[16] Cf. the French: "Un perroquet, ils sont tombés sur un bec de perroquet" (99).

augment the hideousness of his situation: "If I could speak and yet say nothing really nothing? Then I might escape being gnawed to death as by an old satiated rat, and my little tester-bed along with me, a cradle, or be gnawed to death not so fast, in my old cradle, and the torn flesh have time to knit, as in the Caucuses before being torn again. But it seems impossible to speak and yet say nothing, you think you have succeeded, but you always overlook something, a little yes, a little no, enough to exterminate a regiment of dragoons" (303).

Worm's creator transfers some of his own torment to his surrogate. He takes a sardonic pleasure in urging the "delegates" to use rats to chase Worm from his Eden and force him into existence. This exhortation is doubly absurd because the "delegates" themselves are compared to rats and because Worm is potentially another rat-"delegate": "... I'd set the rats on him, water-rats, sewer-rats, they're the best, oh not too many, a dozen to a dozen and a half, that might help him to make up his mind to get going, and what an introduction, to his future attributes" (371). [17]

The metaphor of the hyena is also used to characterize the nature and function of the "delegates." Like the rats, the hyenas feed off the substance of the Unnamable. Their inhuman howls not only mock the Unnamable's efforts to escape their words, they are the words he uses. To abandon his quest for self is to silence them, to submit to language; to continue it is to perpetuate their existence. And the same paradox remains: the search for self necessarily exiles the Unnamable from the void where he has always been — his

---

[17] An earlier image depicting the rat-"delegates" gnawing away at Worm with their words does not appear in the translation. The original passage reads: "... ils n'espèrent que ça durera, c'est un bon fromage, ils ont l'esprit ailleurs, hommes-rats, en appelant Jude..." (153). Figuratively, "un bon fromage" means "a soft job." But Beckett keeps the literal meaning of the expression as well, "a good cheese," by using it in conjunction with his depiction of the "delegates" as rats. The double meaning has not been carried over into the English: "... it's a soft job, they hope things will continue as they are, their thoughts wander as they call on Jude..." (362).

stable and his sanctuary: "... there is nothing else, let us be lucid for once, nothing else but what happens to me, such as speaking, and such as seeking, and which cannot happen to me, which prowl around me ... like hyenas screetching and laughing, no, no better, I've shut my doors against them, I'm not at home to anything ... perhaps that's how I'll find silence and peace at last, by opening my doors and letting myself be devoured, they'll stop howling, they'll start eating, the maws now howling" (391).

God is a necessary invention that springs from the Unnamable's revolt against language. "In the beginning was the Word," the first verse of the Gospel According to St. John relates, "and the Word was with God, and the Word was God." In his attempt to use the word to "uncreate" the universe and restore the void, the Unnamable, unable to be his own God, projects a deity whom he posits as the source of his torment. In his relation to that Godot-like God — whose angels are the "delegates" — the Unnamable portrays himself not as a man created in God's image but as a fish kept dangling on the line by a supreme fisherman — as he is kept dangling on the threshold of the void. The bait in question has been language — the words the Unnamable thought would end his suffering but have only perpetuated it by producing Mahood, Worm (perfect food for a fish!) and the Unnamable as narrator: "The essential is to go on squirming forever on the end of the line, as long as there are waters and banks and ravening in heaven a sporting God to plague his creature, per pro his chosen shits. I've swallowed three hooks and am still hungry" (338).

Whether a fish or a dog or a rat in his diverse incarnations, the Unnamable is forced to become something less than human: "Pupil Mahood, repeat after me, Man is a higher mammal. I couldn't" (337). The gift of language — that which makes man unique in the animal kingdom — dehumanizes him. Like a wild animal in the zoo that finds an outlet for its restless energy by endlessly pacing round and round in its cage, the Unnamable is condemned to turn within his "parlour," condemned to the ceaseless self-proliferation that is the creation of literature: "... I'm something quite different, a quite different thing, a wordless thing in an empty place, a hard shut dry black cold place, where nothing stirs, nothing speaks, and that I listen, and that I seek, like a caged beast born of caged beasts born of caged beasts born of caged beasts born in a cage and dead in a cage, born and then dead, born in a cage and then dead in a cage, in a word like a beast, in one of their words, like such a beast, and that I seek, like such a beast ..." (386-387).

V

The fundamental image that emerges from an examination of the animals inhabiting the trilogy is that of the animal victim. The web of comparisons and analogies that associates men and animals in the three novels plainly reveals that Beckett's protagonists are likewise victims: of a universe tormenting them for reasons unknown; of the other members of the species, their fellow men, who are quick to punish the weak and cast out the misfit; and of a language separating them from their essential reality. In the world of the trilogy, man's supposed dominion over the animals seems a vain notion.

This is the basis for a view of man that is, nonetheless, far from indifferent or nihilistic. However sardonic or cynical Molloy or Malone or Mahood may be with regard to their respective existences or those of other men, their sensitivity to the plight of the animals — their "fellow-convicts" — remains unshaken. Their attitude points toward the presence of yet another, and more inclusive, sensitivity to the inexplicable ubiquity of suffering — that of Beckett or his persona. However harsh his portrayal of existence may be, his sympathy and tenderness are extended to those who bear the burden of that suffering — to the animals who are surely innocent and, through them, indirectly to man, whose innocence is perhaps doubtful but whose torment, that of the wanderer and that of the wanderer-turned-artist, is no less real. Moreover, it is this tenderness and this sympathy that enable Beckett to evoke in the reader a response that does not depend on the nature of the animal. A house-fly, normally considered a disgusting and loathsome insect, can become the object of pity and compassion.

Within the novels of the trilogy Beckett has established a modern bestiary. Unlike the popular medieval bestiary, which took animals, both real and imagined, and interpreted their characteristics allegorically according to a Christian framework, revealing them as links in a chain of being that stretched to God and as an integral part of the unity He had created, Beckett's bestiary, far removed from such lofty conceptions, reveals no order and no higher truth made manifest in the varied forms of life.

Although Beckett often draws upon traditional symbols, such as the lamb or the dog, his use of animal imagery suggests above all a figurative language: to lead a dog's life, work like a horse, die like flies, be led like lambs to the slaughter, etc. In the course of our everyday conversation, this figurative language is banal and colorless. Beckett recreates it in the trilogy, gives it a new vitality and a new urgency by making it a concrete representation of man's destiny. In so doing, he transforms clichés into a trenchant and poetic statement of the human condition.

CONCLUSION

"THE ONLY FERTILE RESEARCH," Beckett wrote in *Proust*, "is excavatory, immersive, a contraction of the spirit, a descent" (48). And he continues: "The artist is active by negatively shrinking from the nullity of circumferential phenomena, drawn into the core of the eddy" (48). Each of the trilogy's author-protagonists — and, in particular, the Unnamable — has accepted these concepts as fundamental, not only as aesthetic criteria but as existential and epistemological ones as well. That is to say, the artist's function corresponds to his concept of self and world, means and ends coincide. Looking at the trilogy as a whole, these closely related processes of shrinking, contraction, and descent give the trilogy a particular shape, that of a three-dimensional spiral coiling ever more tightly around itself.

Near the vanishing point of that spiral we can situate the Unnamable, the *terminus ad quem* of the trilogy and, as we look outward from his vantage point, its source.[1] Like Echo — whose legend inspired Beckett's first collection of poetry, *Echo's Bones and Other Precipitates*, the Unnamable has been reduced to a disembodied voice, having sloughed off the narrators of the earlier volumes in whom he had assumed bodily guise. Through these diverse incarnations he has failed to accede to the empty core of the eddy (the vanishing point of the spiral, the center of the circle); or, what amounts to the same thing, he has failed

---

[1] The Unnamable is similarly the source of the novels that precede the trilogy. Our remarks concerning his role as creator are limited to the latter.

to descend to the deepest zone of consciousness, where the self is a dimensionless point in the void. Having become a voice he must make two painful acknowledgements. First, he is somehow still enmeshed in the phenomenal world, a world from which the essential self remains, by its very nature, absent. Thus his initial questions: "Where now? Who now? When now? Unquestioning. I, say I. Unbelieving. Questions, hypotheses, call them that. Keep going, going on, call that going, call that on" (291). That these questions still need to be answered leads to the Unnamable's second admission. He is afraid that if he continues to speak — though he must continue — he will return once more to the fictions he has rejected and never speak of himself: "And yet I am afraid . . . of what my words will do to me . . . yet again. Is there really nothing new to try? (303).

Before we explore the Unnamable's present dilemma and the manner in which it reflects back upon the entire structure of the trilogy, we must re-examine what he has already "tried." The same processes that shape the trilogy as a whole shape *Molloy* and *Malone Dies*, individually and taken together, and lead inexorably back to the Unnamable.

Molloy marks the greatest departure of the Unnamable from his self, his most profound involvement in "circumferential phenomena," his ascension to the uppermost strata of consciousness — the level closest to external reality.[2] Here the emphasis is on what we might call the "horizontal" dimension of the quest, the macrocosm: Molloy's journey to his mother's room, Moran's search for Molloy. Both protagonists can be considered, from our present perspective, "vice-existers" of the Unnamable, who will later, not having properly served their creator, take their place among the dead satellites than encircle him.

The two-part structure of *Molloy* represents one essential element of contraction — the merging (though never

---

[2] Cf. Beckett's topography of the mind in the Sixth Chapter of *Murphy*.

completed) of these two "vice-existers" into one. As we have noted, when viewed simultaneously, the two halves of the novel reveal Molloy drawing closer to the self as Moran draws closer to Molloy. The point at which they meet and become one lies within the Unnamable, within the self of which Molloy and Moran are projections in space and time. They constitute two faces, two fictional masks of a single protagonist who, as long as the respective journeys of Molloy and Moran are not terminated, remains nameless. Those journeys introduce us as well to the "vertical" dimension of the quest: the abstraction of the protagonist from the macrocosm and his withdrawal into the microcosm — the inner space where true and unending felicity may be found, where fiction replaces life, where perhaps the Unnamable and his "vice-existers" may coincide.

These broader manifestations of shrinking, contraction, and descent are, as I have tried to demonstrate, grounded in certain patterns of imagery. Each of the patterns we have examined tends toward an ultimate reduction that, if realized, would end the Unnamable's quest with *Molloy.* Three of our patterns, those dealing with quantitative entities — space, movement, and light — readily manifest this reductive tendency. The other two — softness and animals — evince a somewhat different, though parallel, diminution. Withdrawal from the macrocosm should, ideally, obviate the threat of absorption and eliminate the cruelty and suffering of existence as portrayed through the animal imagery. However, it becomes apparent in *Molloy* that this imagery needs no support in reality to sustain it, that it is perpetuated in and through language which is a mirror of the phenomenal world. Thus the microcosm reveals itself to be an imperfect refuge as long as it is not "language-tight."

Though a failure, the elaboration of *Molloy* might be considered an experiment of sorts in that it furnishes the Unnamable with a number of insights into the relationship between self, language, and fiction. These will increase in scope and explicitness as the Unnamable continues his

quest, as the creation of the trilogy becomes more and
more the subject of the trilogy. Concomitant with this
process there emerges an artistic consciousness that will
grow increasingly refined, increasingly aware of its own
possibilities and impossibilities — and finally turn against
itself.[3] Molloy condemns the dead words that cannot seize
a self outside of time and space. Moran rejects his "gallery
of moribunds" as the Unnamable will later reject the
"moribunds" of the trilogy. The separation between Moran
throwing off the shackles of his bourgeois existence in
order to become the one he seeks and realize him artistical-
ly and the Unnamable trapped in his "parlour" contains
the entire space of the trilogy. Its three volumes will decrease this distance to a minimum without, however, eliminating it completely.

"There will not be much more," the Unnamable announces in his "preambule," "on the subject of Malone,
from whom there is nothing further to be hoped" (202). Of
all his incarnations in the first two volumes of the trilogy,
it is Malone who most haunts his creator as he turns, im-
passable, around him. It was Malone who brought the Unnamable closest to the end of his quest, who, having
withdrawn from the macrocosm, sunk into the depths of
the consciousness so as to give birth to the self, the "dark
stranger" whose presence he somehow felt within him.

Malone's beginning his narration at the point where
Molloy left off explicitly links the two novels and indicates
that the "vertical" dimension has become of primary concern. Malone's avowal that he is the creator of Molloy and
Moran turns the trilogy inward. The linking of *Molloy*
and *Malone Dies* through the device of overlapping narrators causes them to converge toward the last volume of
the trilogy, in which the Unnamable will cast aside his

---

[3] Ruby Cohn remarks: "*Molloy* shows the making of the artist,
Malone Dies the artist making, and *The Unnamable* the artist's
reflection upon art and the artist." *Samuel Beckett: The Comic
Gamut* (New Brunswick, New Jersey: Rutgers University Press,
1962), p. 118.

surrogate inventors and emerge as the trilogy's prime mover. Malone incorporates the knowledge of his predecessors and goes beyond it. Not only is he aware of the inadequacy of language but he is also aware that his existence in time and space can be transmuted into a proliferation of fictional characters which exist at a lesser or farther remove from the self. Of course, this fragmentation of the personality is the same process that animates the trilogy as a whole. The relating of fiction, a temporal phenomenon, can thus become a means of liberation through a stripping away of these excrescences that cling to the self.

Within this framework our imagery patterns take a curious turn. The spiral expands as it contracts. The Unnamable progressively disengages himself from his "vice-exister" as the latter casts off his "homunculi" (for the Unnamable, "vice-existers" twice removed) by narrating his life away. Thus Malone becomes a means of killing time in order to bring into existence a timeless self. The trilogy recreates itself in order to decreate itself. Sapo-Macmann takes us back to Moran and Molloy, to C and A. We return to the space of the voyager and to his varied movements, to the light of day, to absorbent landscapes and sticky female flesh, to encounters with animals. At the same time, Malone's dwindling existence is portrayed through a continuation of the reduction within these patterns begun in *Molloy*. But when they have finally disappeared, the Unnamable still has no name. Thus we come back to our starting point, to those fundamental questions whose answers could not be found in *Molloy* and *Malone Dies*. The Unnamable must somehow answer them and capture the elusive self without recreating, at least in some minimal form, the same old imagery.

There is indeed something new to try. The Unnamable denies that he is responsible for *Molloy* and *Malone Dies* and attributes their creation to someone else: "He must have travelled, he whose voice it is, he must have seen, with his eyes, a man or two, a thing or two, been aloft in the light, or else heard tales, travellers found him and told

him tales, that proves my innocence ..." (403). Olga Bernal
views this dissociation from language, this rejection of literature, as a fundamental development in the evolution of
Beckett's novels: "The evolution from *Murphy* to *How It Is*
consists of the gradual transformation of the traditional
narrator into a quoter [citeur]. One who quotes states
nothing, affirms nothing, says nothing of himself — he
quotes." [4]

That *he* upon whom the Unnamable places the burden
of his past failures and his present inability to be the self
that was supposedly liberated at the conclusion of *Malone
Dies* is a convenient pronoun, a pseudo-*I* to replace the *I*
the Unnamable cannot say. *They* and *you* are similarly
employed. These pronouns are also objectified. First there
are the "delegates," who inform the Unnamable about those
things of which — if he is outside language — he can know
nothing: "The things they have told me! About men, the
light of day. I refused to believe them. But some of it has
stuck. But when, through what channels, did I communicate with these gentlemen? Did they intrude on me here?
No, no one has ever intruded on me here" (297). Secondly,
there is Mahood, ex-"delegate" turned "vice-exister" who
usurps the role of creator and "heaps stories on the [Un-
namable's] head" (309). Mahood might even be held responsible for the entire trilogy, in addition to his own story
and that of Worm.

The necessary result of this decentralization of the Unnamable, this evasion of his solitary confrontation with
words, can only produce a return to the earlier volumes of
the trilogy. Familiar patterns of imagery begin to reappear.
Mahood in particular, but the "delegates" and Worm as
well, exist through their recreation, born in the microcosm
of language, born in the words that compose the voice. The
beacon of creation that illuminates the Unnamable's space
takes us back to that "life aloft in the light." Mahood the

---

[4] Olga Bernal, *Langage et fiction dans le roman de Beckett*
(Paris: Gallimard, 1969), p. 82.

voyager and Worm, the speechless blur in the void, now become the two poles between which we can situate all the "vice-existers" that have preceded them. The reductive process that brought the Unnamable to where he is is thus recapitulated once more.

Although he will continue to deny that his self lies within the words he uses, the Unnamable recognizes the absurdity of his refusal to accept the burden of creation. He is a voice in the wilderness of language; there has never been anyone else but himself and his inventions. As we know, Mahood and Worm are only pseudo-selves with whom the Unnamable has failed to coincide. In dismissing them, as he dismissed their predecessors, in order to speak about himself he traps himself once more in the solipcism that has perpetuated his quest. He must speak if he is to find the self, but the voice in search of its silent essence can only tell stories about itself.

And the stories the voice will tell will be the same old stories, whose bits and pieces will be sifted and resifted. Perhaps the *I* of the Unnamable is indeed somewhere within them, scattered among the *he's* and *they's*. Although the Unnamable has denied this possibility, there is no way of being certain. Whatever the case, the voice has no choice but to continue:

> ... I use them all, all the words they showed me, there were columns of them, oh the strange glow all of a sudden, they were on lists with images opposite, I must have forgotten them, I must have mixed them up, these nameless images I have, these imageless names, these windows I should perhaps rather call doors, at least by some other name, and this word man, which is perhaps not the right one for the thing I see when I hear it, but an instant, an hour, and so on, how can they be represented, a life, how could that be made clear to me, here in the dark, I call that the dark, perhaps it's azure, blank words, but I use them, they keep coming back, all those they showed me, all those I remember, I need them all to be able to go on.... (407-408)

There is no beginning and no end to the Unnamable's discourse, unless it be the arbitrary first page of *Molloy* and last page of *The Unnamable*. The trilogy may thus be considered a block of words torn from the continuum of language as part of a never-ending search for silence.

SELECTED CRITICISM AND COMMENTARY
ON THE TRILOGY

Barnard, G. C. *Samuel Beckett: A New Approach.* London: J. M. Dent, 1970.

Bernal, Olga. *Langage et fiction dans le roman de Beckett.* Paris: Gallimard, 1969.

Blanchot, Maurice. "Où Maintenant? Qui Maintenant?" *Le livre à venir.* Paris: Gallimard, 1959. Pp. 256-264.

Bollnow, Otto F. "Samuel Beckett." *Antares,* 4 (March 1956), 31-36; (April 1956), 36-38; (June 1956), 42-43.

Brée, Germaine. "L'Etrange Monde des 'grands articulés'." In *Configuration critique de Samuel Beckett,* edited by Melvin J. Friedman. Paris: Minard, 1964. Pp. 83-97.

Brick, Allan. "The Madman in His Cell: Joyce, Beckett, Nabokov and the stereotypes." *Massachusetts Review,* 1 (October 1959), 40-55.

Chambers, Ross. "Samuel Beckett and the Padded Cell." *Meanjin Quarterly,* 21 (December 1962), 451-462.

———. "Beckett's Brinkmanship." In *Samuel Beckett: A Collection of Critical Essays,* edited by Martin Esslin. Englewood Cliffs, New Jersey: Spectrum Books, 1965. Pp. 152-168.

Champigny, Robert. "Les Aventures de la première personne." In *Configuration critique de Samuel Beckett,* edited by Melvin J. Friedman. Paris: Minard, 1964. Pp. 117-130.

———. "Adventures of the First Person." In *Samuel Beckett Now,* edited by Melvin J. Friedman. Chicago: University of Chicago Press, 1970. Pp. 119-128.

Cmarada, Geraldine. "*Malone Dies*: A Round of Consciousness." *Symposium,* 14 (Fall 1960), 199-212.

Coe, Richard N. "Le Dieu de Samuel Beckett." *Cahiers de la compagnie Renaud-Barrault,* no. 44 (1963), 6-36.

———. *Samuel Beckett.* New York: Grove Press, 1964.

Cohn, Ruby. "A Note on Beckett, Dante, and Geulincx." *Comparative Literature,* 12 (Winter 1960), 93-94.

———. *Samuel Beckett: The Comic Gamut.* New Brunswick, New Jersey: Rutgers University Press, 1962.

———. "Philosophical Fragments in the Works of Samuel Beckett." *Criticism,* 6 (Winter 1964), 33-43.

Delye, Huguette. *Samuel Beckett, ou la philosophie de l'absurde.* Aix-en-Provence: Publications des Annales de la Faculté des Lettres, 1960.

"Dossier de presse de *Molloy*. In *Molloy* by Samuel Beckett. Paris: U. G. E., 10/18, 1963. Pp. 255-286.

Dreyfus, Dina. "Vraies et fausses énigmes." *Mercure de France,* 331 (October 1957), 268-285.

Driver, Tom F. "Beckett by the Madeleine." *Columbia University Forum,* 4 (Summer 1961), 21-25. ◆

Duckworth, Colin, ed. *En attendant Godot* by Samuel Beckett. London: George G. Harrap, 1966. Pp. vii-xliv.

Erickson, John D. "Objects and Systems in the Novels of Samuel Beckett." *L'Esprit créateur,* 7 (Summer 1967), 113-122.

Esslin, Martin. "Samuel Beckett." In *The Novelist as Philosopher: Studies in French Fiction, 1935-1960,* edited by John Cruickshank. London: Oxford University Press, 1962. Pp. 128-146.

———, ed. "Introduction." *Samuel Beckett: A Collection of Critical Essays.* Englewood Cliffs, New Jersey: Spectrum Books, 1965. Pp. 128-146.

Federman, Raymond. "Samuel Beckett ou le bonheur en enfer." *Symposium,* 21 (Spring 1967), 14-21.

———. "Le Bonheur chez Samuel Beckett." *Esprit,* 362 (1967), 90-96.

Fitch, Brian T. "Narrateur et narration dans la trilogie romanesque de Samuel Beckett: *Molloy, Malone meurt, L'Innommable.*" *Bulletin des Jeunes Romanistes,* no. 3 (May 1961), 13-20.

Fletcher, John. *The Novels of Samuel Beckett.* London: Chatto and Windus, 1964.

———. "Samuel Beckett and the Philosophers." *Comparative Literature,* 17 (Winter 1965), 43-56.

———. *Samuel Beckett's Art.* London: Chatto and Windus, 1967.

Friedman, Melvin J. "The Novels of Samuel Beckett: An Amalgam of Joyce and Proust." *Comparative Literature,* 12 (Winter 1960), 47-58.

———. "Samuel Beckett and the Nouveau Roman." *Wisconsin Studies in Contemporary Literature,* 1 (Spring-Summer 1960), 22-36.

———. "Les Romans de Samuel Beckett et la tradition du grotesque." In *Situation 3, Un Nouveau Roman: recherches et traditions,* edited by J. H. Mathews. Paris: Minard, 1964. Pp. 31-50.

———, ed. *Configuration critique de Samuel Beckett.* Paris: Minard, 1964.

———. "Molloy's 'Sacred' Stones." *Romance Notes,* 9 (1967), 8-11.

———, ed. *Samuel Beckett Now.* Chicago: University of Chicago Press, 1970.

Frye, Northrop. "The Nightmare Life in Death." *Hudson Review,* 13 (Autumn 1960), 442-448.

Gessner, Niklaus. *Die Unzulänglichkeit der Sprache: Eine Untersuchung über Formzerfall und Beziehungslosigkeit.* Zurich: Juris Verlag, 1957.

Glicksberg, Charles I. "Samuel Beckett's World of Fiction." *Arizona Quarterly,* 18 (Spring 1962), 32-47.

154   THE LIFE AFTER BIRTH

Greenberg, Alvin. "The Novel of Disintegration: Paradoxical Impossibility in Contemporary Fiction." *Wisconsin Studies in Contemporary Literature*, 7 (Winter-Spring 1966), 103-124.
Gregory, Horace. *The Dying Gladiators of Samuel Beckett and Other Essays*. New York: Grove Press, 1961. Pp. 165-176.
Hansen-Löve, Friedrich. "Samuel Beckett oder die Einübung ins Nichts," *Hochland*, 50 (October 1957), 36-46.
Hassan, Ihab. *The Literature of Silence: Henry Miller and Samuel Beckett*. New York: Knopf, 1967.
Hayman, David. "*Molloy* or the Quest for Meaninglessness: A Global Interpretation." In *Samuel Beckett Now*, edited by Melvin J. Friedman. Chicago: University of Chicago Press, 1970. Pp. 129-156.
Heppenstall, Rayner. *The Fourfold Tradition: Notes on the French and English Literature with some Ethnological and Historical Asides*. London: Barrie and Rockliff, 1961. Pp. 254-265.
Hoffman, Frederick J. *Samuel Beckett: The Language of Self*. Carbondale, Illinois: Southern Illinois University Press, 1962.
Jacobsen, Josephine and Mueller, William R. *The Testament of Samuel Beckett*. New York: Hill and Wang, 1964.
Janvier, Ludovic. *Pour Samuel Beckett*. Paris: Editions de Minuit, 1966.
————. "Beckett et ses fables." *Livre de France*, no. 1 (January 1967), 4-13.
————. *Beckett par lui-même*. Paris: Seuil, 1969.
Kenner, Hugh. *Samuel Beckett: A Critical Study*. New York: Grove Press, 1961. New edition with a supplementary chapter. Berkeley: University of California Press, 1968.
————. *Flaubert, Joyce and Beckett: The Stoic Comedians*. Boston: Beacon Press, 1962.
Kern, Edith. "Moran-Molloy: The Hero as Author." *Perspective*, 11 (Autumn 1959), 183-192.
————. "Black Humour: The Pockets of Lemuel Gulliver and Samuel Beckett." In *Samuel Beckett Now*, edited by Melvin J. Friedman. Chicago: University of Chicago Press, 1970. Pp. 89-102.
————. *Existential Thought and Fictional Technique: Kierkegaard, Sartre, Beckett*. New Haven, Connecticut: Yale University Press, 1970.
Lee, Warren. "The Bitter Pill of Samuel Beckett." *Chicago Review*, 10 (Winter 1957), 77-87.
Leventhal, A. J. "The Beckett Hero." *Critique: Studies in Modern Fiction*, 7 (Winter 1964-65), 18-35.
Loy, Robert. "Things in Recent French Literature." *PMLA*, 71 (March 1956), 17-19.
Macksey, Richard. "The Artist in the Labyrinth: Design or Dasein." *Modern Language Notes*, 77 (May 1962), 239-256.
Marissel, André. *Beckett*. Paris: Editions Universitaires, 1963.
Mayoux, Jean-Jacques. "Samuel Beckett et l'univers parodique." *Vivants Piliers*. Paris: Julliard, 1960. Pp. 271-291.
————. *Über Samuel Beckett*. Frankfurt am Main: Suhrkamp Verlag, 1966.
Mercier, Vivian. "Beckett and the Search for Self." *New Republic*, 19 September 1955, pp. 20-21.

Mercier, Vivian. "The Mathematical Limit." *Nation*, 14 February 1959, pp. 144-145.

Miller, J. Hillis. "The Anonymous Walkers." *Nation*, 23 April 1960, pp. 351-354.

Morse, Mitchell J. "The Contemplative Life According to Samuel Beckett." *Hudson Review*, 15 (Winter 1962-63), 512-524.

Nadeau, Maurice. "Samuel Beckett ou le droit de silence." *Les Temps Modernes*, 8 (January 1952), 1273-82.

Oates, Joyce Carol. "The Trilogy of Samuel Beckett." *Renascence*, 14 (Spring 1962), 160-165.

O'Hara, J. D., ed. *Twentieth Century Interpretations of Molloy, Malone Dies, The Unnamable*. Englewood Cliffs, New Jersey: Spectrum Books, 1970.

Onimus, Jean. *Beckett*. Bruges: Desclée de Brouwer, 1968.

Oxenhandler, Neal. "The Metaphor of a Metaphor in La Nausée." *Chicago Review*, 15 (Summer-Autumn 1962), 47-54.

Pingaud, Bernard. "*Molloy* douze ans après." *Les Temps Modernes*, 18 (January 1963), 1283-1300.

Pouillon, Jean. "*Molloy*." *Les Temps Modernes*, 7 (July 1951), 184-86.

Rickels, Milton. "Existential Themes in Beckett's *Unnamable*." *Criticism*, 4 (Spring 1962), 134-147.

Riva, Raymond T. "Beckett and Freud." *Criticism*, 12 (Spring 1970), 120-132.

Scott, Nathan. *Samuel Beckett*. London: Bowes and Bowes, 1965.

Solomon, Philip H. "Samuel Beckett's *Molloy*: A Dog's Life." *French Review*, 41 (October 1967), 84-91.

————. "Lousse and Molloy: Beckett's Bower of Bliss." *Australian Journal of French Studies*, 6 (1969), 65-81.

————. "Samuel Beckett's *L'Innommable:* The Space of Fiction." *Forum for Modern Language Studies*, 7 (January 1971), 83-91.

Strauss, Walter A. "Dante's Belacqua and Beckett's Tramps." *Comparative Literature*, 11 (Summer 1959), 250-261.

Sypher, Wylie. "The Anonymous Self: A Defensive Humanism." In *Loss of the Self in Modern Literature and Art*. New York: Vintage Books, 1962. Pp. 147-165.

Tagliaferri, Aldo. *Beckett e l'iperdeterminazione letteraria*. Milan: Feltrinelli, 1967.

Tindall, William York. "Beckett's Bums." *Critique: Studies in Modern Fiction*, 2 (Spring-Summer 1958), 3-15.

————. *Samuel Beckett*. New York and London: Columbia University Press, 1964.

Vigée, Claude. "Les Artistes de la Faim." *Comparative Literature*, 9 (Spring 1957), 97-117.

Webb, Eugene. *Samuel Beckett: A Study of His Novels*. Seattle: University of Washington Press, 1970.

Wellershof, Dieter. "Failure of an Attempt at De-Mythologization: Samuel Beckett's Novels." In *Samuel Beckett: A Collection of Critical Essays*, edited by Martin Esslin. Englewood Cliffs, New Jersey: Spectrum Books, 1965. Pp. 92-107.

Wilson, Colin. "Samuel Beckett." In *The Strength to Dream: Literature and the Imagination*. Boston: Houghton Mifflin, 1962. Pp. 86-91.